Who's the Blonde That Married What's-His-Name?

Carol Boswell and Lenore Skenazy

Who's the Blonde That Married What's-His-Name?

The Ultimate Tip-of-the-Tongue Test of Everything You Know You Know— But Can't Remember Right Now

A Perigee Book

A PERIGEE BOOK
Published by the Penguin Group
Penguin Group (USA) Inc.
375 Hudson Street, New York, New York 10014, USA

Penguin Group (Canada), 90 Eglinton Avenue East, Suite 700, Toronto, Ontario M4P 2Y3, Canada (a division of Pearson Penguin Canada Inc.) • Penguin Books Ltd., 80 Strand, London WC2R 0RL, England • Penguin Group Ireland, 25 St. Stephen's Green, Dublin 2, Ireland (a division of Penguin Books Ltd.) • Penguin Group (Australia), 250 Camberwell Road, Camberwell, Victoria 3124, Australia (a division of Pearson Australia Group Pty. Ltd.) • Penguin Books India Pvt. Ltd., 11 Community Centre, Panchsheel Park, New Delhi—110 017, India • Penguin Group (NZ), 67 Apollo Drive, Rosedale, North Shore 0632, New Zealand (a division of Pearson New Zealand Ltd.) • Penguin Books (South Africa) (Pty.) Ltd., 24 Sturdee Avenue, Rosebank, Johannesburg 2196, South Africa

Penguin Books Ltd., Registered Offices: 80 Strand, London WC2R 0RL, England

While the author has made every effort to provide accurate telephone numbers and Internet addresses at the time of publication, neither the publisher nor the author assumes any responsibility for errors, or for changes that occur after publication. Further, the publisher does not have any control over and does not assume any responsibility for author or third-party websites or their content.

First edition: June 2009

Library of Congress Cataloging-in-Publication Data

Boswell, Carol, 1945–
    Who's the blonde that married what's-his-name? : the ultimate tip-of-the-tongue test of everything you know you know—but can't remember right now / Carol Boswell and Lenore Skenazy.
        p.   cm.
    "A Perigee book."
    ISBN 978-0-399-53498-0
    1. Popular culture—Miscellanea. 2. Questions and answers. I. Skenazy, Lenore. II. Title.
AG195.B65 2009
030—dc23   2009002641

PRINTED IN THE UNITED STATES OF AMERICA

10 9 8 7 6 5 4 3 2 1

Most Perigee books are available at special quantity discounts for bulk purchases for sales promotions, premiums, fund-raising, or educational use. Special books, or book excerpts, can also be created to fit specific needs. For details, write: Special Markets, Penguin Group (USA) Inc., 375 Hudson Street, New York, New York 10014.

Contents

Who's the Blonde That Married What's-His-Name?

Introduction

You Know You Know It . . .

It's right there on the tip of your tongue—the name of the guy in that action movie. You know—*what's-his-name*. With the long leather jacket. He's got a funny first name. It starts with a K, right? Kyle? Kermit? Kiefer! Wait, that's the other guy. Try again. It's . . . it's . . .

It's just incredible. This groping-for-the-answer, I've-almost-got-it phenomenon is so universal that in almost every language, people describe it the same, frustrated way. They say the word they're looking for is right on their lips or at the back of their throat. But for most of us—"It's on the tip of my tongue." (Keanu Reeves! It's Keanu Reeves!)

Who's the Blonde That Married What's-His-Name?: The Ultimate Tip-of-the-Tongue Test of Everything You Know You Know—But Can't Remember Right Now is the world's first quiz book that puts all of that answer-groping we do in our daily lives to good use. Think of it as Mad Libs with a mental block. Or maybe it's more Six Degrees of Separation, since all the clues are connected in wacky ways. You'll find questions on everything from pop culture to history to kids' stuff, posed every which tip-of-the-tongue way, using every weird word association trick you use in real life to try to remember all kinds of information. The more blanks you fill in, the more points you score.

Psychologists who study the tip-of-the-tongue phenomenon—a hot new research topic—say kids as young as six experience it. By college, people are tongue-tipping about two times a week and it just goes up (or down) from there. That's because far from being organized like an orderly filing cabinet, the brain stores information like a kooky old professor shuffling stacks of random papers on his desk, trying to find that *one scrap* with the answer on it.

Or think of it this way: Information about even a single topic is scattered around your brain like dirty laundry around a teenager's bedroom—one sock under the bed, the other in the fish tank. (How did it get there?) So when it's time for your brain to locate the information you need—the capital of Florida, perhaps, or the last name of your first-grade teacher—there are many different avenues it can take to try to scrounge up the correct information, from thinking of words that sound similar (but have entirely different meanings) to thinking of what the answer *isn't*.

The good news is that while the mechanics of the tip-of-the-tongue phenomenon are still under examination, it's possible that the more you play with word associations, the more pathways you have to access those words when you need them. That means *Who's the Blonde That Married What's-His-Name?* may—we hope!—even be a memory booster.

Based on all the crazy ways our brains retrieve information, we've developed four different kinds of quizzes:

TONGUE TIPPERS take you on a wild ride from the tip of your tongue to the crannies of your brain and back, using word associations, strange connections, visual clues, trivia—everything but that thing in the kitchen that the water comes out of. Your job is to fill in all the blanks in each Tongue Tipper. For instance:

_____ that married _____ whose last name
WHO'S THE BLONDE   WHAT'S-HIS-NAME

sounds like a ___, but then they split and she was in that
              BIRD

_____ that totally revived the career of the _____
SUPER-HIP MOVIE   DANCING

_____ before he played a woman in that _____ by the
SCIENTOLOGIST   MUSICAL

_____?
BALTIMORE ODDBALL

Now, of course, you might not remember the BLONDE's name immediately. (Especially if you're blond!) (Sorry.) But if you start thinking about the DANCING SCIENTOLOGIST you may think, "Tom Cruise? But he's not a dancer. Oh wait—it's John Travolta!" And remembering Travolta helps you remember that movie that really did bring him back from the Hollywood dead was _Pulp Fiction_. And his co-star was that sexy blonde— Uma Thurman—who was married to that guy with a bird name. Hawk, right? Ethan Hawke!

Okay! You've filled in a bunch of the blanks already. And meantime, you remember that Travolta bravely decided to play the mom in _Hairspray_, the original version of which was directed by that funny, transvestite-obsessed Baltimore guy John Waters. And you have now filled in every single blank.

Congrats. We'll tell you how to score in a second. But first, here are the other types of quizzes you'll find in the book:

SOUND ALIKES are answers that are connected loosely—very loosely—by similar sounds. Either the words rhyme, or they start with the same letter, or they just sort of sound similar. If you get one or two answers, they will help you figure out the rest simply by wild and free word association. For instance:

Hat with a propeller on top: _____

Easter animal that's not a chick: _____

Clyde's partner: _____

The way Mary-Kate Olsen looks: _____

Now, you may not remember what you call a hat with a propeller on top, but you do recall that Clyde's partner was Bonnie. And that sort of sounds like "beanie," right? So now you've got the hat answer—beanie—and you've got Bonnie, which means the Easter animal is probably not a turtle or an elephant but a bunny. Beanie, Bunny, Bonnie—so what's the way Mary-Kate Olsen looks? Bony!

Beanie, Bunny, Bonnie, Bony

Some of these are really hard (or really silly), so don't beat yourself up if it takes you a while to get the hang of it.

TAKE 10s are groups of, yes, 10 things that share one thing in common. They're 10 redheads, or 10 childhood games, or 10 talking heads that don't shut up on cable—whatever. So if the category is "Doctors" and the clue is "The one who put the cat in the hat," you know the answer is Dr. Seuss. And if the clue is "The one who comes in a can or bottle," well . . . we'll let you figure that one out on your own.

THE ONE THAT'S NOT: Sometimes, the brain works in mysterious ways. Often, it will link information in pairs. So maybe it can't remember the word "Celsius" (and why would it?), but it can remember the word it has forever paired Celsius with. That's why it ends up asking, "What's the one that's not Fahrenheit?"

Or maybe all that the brain can remember about the guy who married that Jennifer actress with the dimples is that he's "the one that's not Matt Damon."

Did you mentally shout, "Ben Affleck"? If so, you get it. Basically, the One That's Not looks into who is sharing lockers in our brain.

Now you're ready to begin.

Play Who's the Blonde? as a thinking game—or drinking game. Play it alone or with friends. Bring it on family trips or to a party and just watch how everyone starts shouting out answers—*Dirty Dancing*! Jim Cramer! Stegosaurus!—when they're not racking their brains, going, "I know I know it, but . . ."

So start playing!

SCORING: Every blank you fill in correctly counts for one point. If you fill in every single blank in a Tongue Tipper, Take 10, Sound Alike, or lighting round of the One That's Not, you get a 5-point bonus. Play till 50 points, or 100, and just remember to take turns. (Unless you're playing solo, at which point taking turns would be strange.) You can check the answer key at the back. But don't cheat!

We've left a couple of pages blank at the end so you can start coming up with your own Tongue Tippers, Sound Alikes, and others. Email your gems to us at www.whostheblondebook.com, and we'll try to include them in the next round.

Okay, you're ready to play. Have whatchamacallit!

Uh, fun.

—*Carol and Lenore*

Reel Life

★ Tongue Tipper ★

1. Who's the _____ who used to be in all
ADORABLE BLONDE

those romantic comedies like the _____ and
SEATTLE ONE

the _____ but then she had
"I'LL HAVE WHAT SHE'S HAVING" ONE

an affair with the _____ and
AUSTRALIAN GUY WITH THE TEMPER

ended up divorced from her _____ whose _____
HUSBAND   BROTHER

is someone, too?

2. Who's the _____ who rode the chariot in that _____
NRA GUY   MOVIE

that sounds like the _____?
STUFF YOU RUB ON SORE MUSCLES

3. What are those _____ the creature in that
CANDIES

_____ ate that sound like the name of the
SPIELBERG MOVIE

_____ who dyed her hair dark to play the
<u>LEGALLY BLONDE BLONDE</u>

___ of the _____ and sang like her, too?
<u>WIFE</u>   <u>GUY IN BLACK</u>

4. What was that _____ where the _____ is the
              <u>TEARJERKER</u>   <u>CUCKOO'S NEST GUY</u>

neighbor of the _____ whose _____ dies?
              <u>MOTHER</u>   <u>DAUGHTER</u>

5. What's that ____ with the _____ that everyone hums
            <u>MOVIE</u>   <u>BANJO THEME</u>

when something perverted is about to happen?

6. Who's _____ famous _____ who directed the
        <u>WHAT'S-HIS-NAME'S</u>   <u>DAUGHTER</u>

_____ that the _____ almost won an
<u>MOVIE IN TOKYO</u>   <u>POCKMARKED COMEDIAN</u>

Oscar for, and it jump-started the career of that _____
                                        <u>BLONDE</u>

who wore underpants in it?

7. What's that _____ with the
            <u>SUMMER RESORT MOVIE IN THE CATSKILLS</u>

_____ and the _____
<u>GUY IN THE TIGHT PANTS</u>   <u>ACTRESS BEFORE HER NOSE JOB</u>

whose _____ was the _Law & Order_ actor and ____
     <u>MOVIE FATHER</u>   <u>REAL-</u>

_____ was the _Cabaret_ guy?
<u>LIFE DAD</u>

8. Who's the _____ who's been
            <u>ACTRESS WITH THE BULGING EYES</u>

with that _____ ever since she fell for him in that
       <u>TALL ACTOR</u>

_____ where she had amazing sex with the
<u>BASEBALL MOVIE</u>

_____?
<u>OTHER GUY</u>

9. What's that ____ in that _____ where the piano

CAFÉ · CLASSIC MOVIE

player isn't supposed to play _____ but he does and

THAT SONG

it enrages _____—the short actor who was

WHAT'S-HIS-NAME

married to the _____—

"PUT YOUR LIPS TOGETHER AND BLOW" ACTRESS

even though in the movie he'll always have Paris with

the _____ who in real life had the affair

BLOND SWEDISH ACTRESS

with the _____ and their _____ was the face

ITALIAN DIRECTOR · DAUGHTER

of Lancôme until they dumped her when she got a

wrinkle?

10. Who's the _____ who married the ____

SUPERSTAR WITH THE BUTT · SKINNY

_____ after she and the _____—who's not the

LATINO SINGER · BOSTON GUY

_____—broke up and then he had a baby or two

HARVARD GUY

with the _____ who can't have a baby

ACTRESS WITH THE DIMPLES

in that _____ about the pregnant sixteen-

SURPRISE HIT MOVIE

year-old?

11. What's that _____ they make summer suits out

PUCKERED COTTON

of, like the one the ____ wears in the _____ with the

ACTOR · MUSICAL

_____ and the _____ who in real life went on

TROMBONE SONG · LISPING KID

to make the _____ and the

MOVIE ABOUT THE OLD PEOPLE IN THE WATER

_____ that isn't the _____, and every-

ONE ABOUT THE MERMAID · ANIMATED ONE

thing else?

12. Who's the _____ who hooked up with the
             BLOND SUPERMODEL

_____ after her relationship with the _____
QUARTERBACK   DEPARTED ACTOR

sank and her last name is like those _____ you see in
                                                      LITTLE PEOPLE

the _____ after the twister when the _____ is told _____
      MOVIE   LITTLE DOG   WHERE

_____?
HE ISN'T ANYMORE

13. Who's the _____ who's obsessed with rose
             USUAL SUSPECTS GUY

petals in that _____ that co-stars the _____
                    SUBURBAN FILM   OLDER HOT

_____ cute _____ who hooked up with him in the
GUY'S   PUG-NOSED WIFE

_____ that sounds like it's about insects?
GANGSTER FLICK

14. What's the _____ with the _____ and the ___
             QUIRKY MOVIE   TITANIC WOMAN   PET

_____ where you go into that machine and forget every-
DETECTIVE

thing, like the really long title of this movie?

15. What's that _____ that sort of sounds
             ISRAELI HAIRDRESSER MOVIE

like that _____ that starred the
             CUTE ACTRESS WHO'S ALWAYS IN REHAB

_____ who sang that _____?
BILLY MADISON GUY   JEWISH HOLIDAY SONG

16. Who's the _____ in that _____ with the little
             GUY WHO PLAYS THE SHRINK   MOVIE

boy who sees dead people that was as popular as the _____
                                                                      ONE THEY

_____ with the people who eat people—
ALWAYS SHOW ON HALLOWEEN

which, by the way, is not the song by _____?
                                                    WHAT'S-HER-NAME

17. What's that _____ that love-struck teens pull apart that's
               FLOWER

not the _____ that the _____
          VALENTINE'S DAY ONE   LADY WHO HELD SALONS IN

____ kept repeating in that _____ in her poem that's
PARIS   FAMOUS QUOTE

_____ that the newspaper tycoon whispers
ALMOST THE SAME WORD

in that _____ by the ____ who got radio listeners
        CLASSIC MOVIE   GUY

scared about the end of the world just like that ____ who
                                                 BIRD

said that _____?
          THING ABOUT THE SKY

★ Take 10 ★

Movies You've Probably Seen I

What's—

1. The _____?
ONE WITH THE SCARY CABBIE

2. The _____?
ONE WITH THE SPORTS AGENT

3. The _____?
ONE WITH THE LIGHT SABERS

4. The _____?
ONE WITH THE FAVA BEANS AND CHIANTI

5. The _____?
ONE WITH THE GUY ON THE BOMB

6. The _____?
ONE WITH "PLASTICS!"

7. The _____?
ONE WTH THE CHICKEN SALAD SANDWICH

8. The _____?
ONE WITH NAPALM

9. The _____?
ONE WITH THE DEAD BASEBALL PLAYERS

10. The _____?
ONE WITH THE ICEBERG

★ Take 10 ★

Movies You've Probably Seen II

What's—

1. The _____?
   ONE WITH THE RAT CHEF

2. The _____?
   ONE WITH THE CORNROWS

3. The _____?
   ONE WITH THE HAIR GEL

4. The _____?
   ONE WITH THE BOILED BUNNY

5. The _____?
   ONE WITH THE DONKEY

6. The _____?
   ONE WITH THE GUY WHO COULDA BEEN A CONTENDER

7. The _____?
   ONE WITH THE PODS

8. The _____?
   ONE WITH THE BOX OF CHOCOLATES

9. The _____?
   ONE WITH THE TWO BIKERS

10. The _____?
    ONE WITH THE SAND

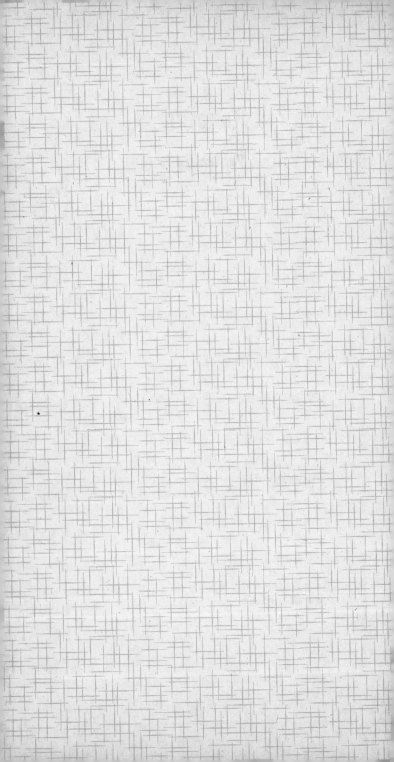

Wide World of Sports

★ Tongue Tipper ★

1. Who was that _____ who said he was the
BASEBALL PLAYER

luckiest guy in the world even though he clearly wasn't?

2. Who's the _____ who won that
FLOATS LIKE A BUTTERFLY GUY

huge _____ a year after he won that
FIGHT IN THE PHILIPPINES

_____ against the _____?
FIGHT IN AFRICA   BOXER WHO BECAME A GRILL

3. What's that _____ that looks like a
OLYMPIC WINTER SPORT

really long version of a ride you'd find at a water

park that's almost as weird as the _____
SPORT WITH THE

_____ that's like an ice version of that _____
BROOMS   GAME

_____ on cruises run by that _____ that
RETIREES PLAY   COMPANY

made people throw up?

4. Who's the _____ who got into that _____
      BASEBALL PLAYER   RELIGION WITH

_____ and hot water with his wife all thanks to the
THE RED STRING

_____?
SINGER WITH THE CONES

5. What's that _____ that's not the
                 SKINNY BOAT THAT'S ALSO A COLOGNE

other _____ that sounds like the _____
      SKINNY BOAT   VOLUPTUOUS MEXICAN

_____?
ACTRESS

6. What's that _____ with the table that
                 STRETCHING EXERCISE CLASS

looks like a torture chamber that's in every fancy gym,

usually near the _____ with the
                CLASS IN THE SWEATY DARK ROOM

loud music and the bikes and the people who think they're

going as fast as the guys in that _____ with the spandex
                                  BIG RACE

and all _____?
        THOSE DRUGS

7. What's that _____ in Japan that sounds like
                 FAT WRESTLING THING

_____?
GRADUATING WITH HIGH HONORS FROM COLLEGE

8. What's the _____ that's in the
                SPORT WITH THE BOOTS AND THE FLIES

_____ that's become so fancy you can't just sit
MOVIE WITH THE RIVER

around in a boat all day like they did in the _____
                                             MOVIE WITH THE

_____ that starred _____ and the _____
POND   JANE'S FATHER   ACTRESS WHOSE HEAD

_____?
ALWAYS SHOOK

9. Who's the _____ whose name sounds like that kind
          QUARTERBACK

of _____ who abused all of those _____
       VAPOR RUB   DOGS THAT AREN'T ALL BAD

and made that _____ even
                    ORGANIZATION THAT THROWS PAINT AT PEOPLE

angrier than usual?

10. Who's the _____—not the
                  WRESTLER WHO BECAME A GOVERNOR

_____—who's less famous than that _____
BODYBUILDER GOVERNOR   TANNED,

_____ who has the same
BLOND WRESTLER WITH THE REALITY SHOW

name as that _____?
                  BIG, GREEN COMIC BOOK CHARACTER

11. What's that _____ that sounds
                   GAME WITH THE NETS ON THE STICKS

like the name of the _____ that prep-
                        SHIRTS WITH THE ALLIGATORS

pies wear, but it's not the _____
                              GAME WITH THE PONIES AND THE STICKS

that's the name of the other shirts that preppies wear?

12. What did they call that ____ the _____
                              SHIP   SURVIVAL OF THE FITTEST GUY

took that was named after the adorable breed that finally

was top dog at the _____ that has all those people
                     BIG ELITIST SHOW

in the stands cheering as loud for dogs as beer guzzlers do

at the _____?
        SPORT WITH THE CARS

13. What's that _____ with the pregnant girl
                   MICHAEL JACKSON SONG

whose name is the same as that feminist _____ who
                                          TENNIS CHAMP

inspired the _____ and the _____
CHAMP WITH THE RUFFLES   ONE WHO CAME

_____?
OUT OF THE CLOSET EARLY ON

14. What's that _____ they put in Chinese food that gives
STUFF

people headaches that has the same initials as that _____
SPORTS

_____ in New York that sounds like it should have a lot
ARENA

of trees and flowers but it's actually ugly and indoors and

has that _____ that the _____ yells at
BASKETBALL TEAM   MALCOLM X DIRECTOR

from the front row?

★ SOUND ALIKES I ★

Fill in the blanks with words that sound alike, more or less. Sometimes less.

1. Implement for writing that usually has an eraser:

_____

Sheet that is cardboard or plastic with cut-out designs:

_____

20/20 anchor with a moustache:

_____

Leaf, shell, or bone from millions of years ago:

_____

2. Thing kids hit with a stick at parties:

_____

All-Star Yankees catcher:

_____

Beethoven's *Moonlight* piece:

_____

Ol' Blue Eyes, may he rest in peace:

_____

3. Unattractive, tent-like dress:

_____

Sound a train makes:

_____

Comma-shaped nut:

_____

Sound of a sneeze:

_____

4. Hat with a propeller on top:

_____

Easter animal that's not a chick:

_____

Clyde's partner:

_____

The way Mary-Kate Olsen looks:

_____

5. What a baby wears at feeding time:

_____

Short, blunt, female haircut:

_____

What goes in a bikini top (singular):

_____

What goes in a bikini bottom:

_____

6. Big continent we get all of our stuff from:

_____

Romanov daughter who might have survived:

_____

What you get before an operation:

_____

What you get when you forget:

_____

7. Modern name for cool witch religion:

_____

Online encyclopedia you can't always trust:

_____

Street where desperate housewives live, also a
climbing vine:

_____

Crazed state of mind:

_____

8. Place where kids go on school trips to look at the stars:

_____

Institution where people go to recuperate:

_____

Someone who doesn't eat meat:

_____

A person who helps others:

_____

9. Italian dish that's usually round, with or without pepperoni, sausage, etc.:

_____

Leaning tower:

_____

Small nut and green ice cream flavor:

_____

Baseball legend who married Marilyn Monroe:

_____

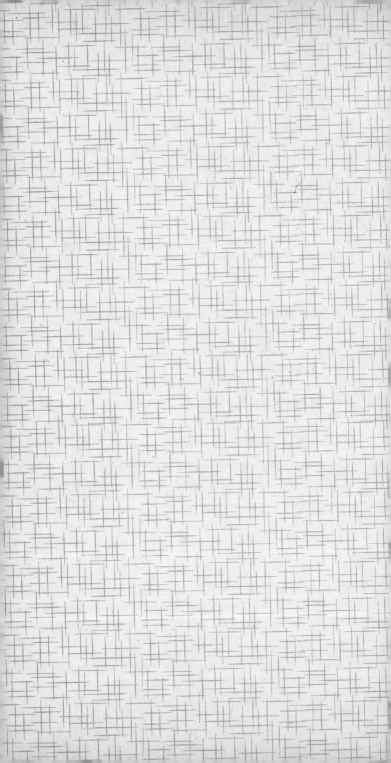

Superstars More or Less

★ Tongue Tipper ★

1. Who's the _____ who was in that _____
  BALD GUY   ACTION MOVIE WITH

_____ who was married to _____
ALL THE SEQUELS   WHAT'S-HER-NAME

_____ before she married the _____?
WITH THE DARK HAIR   PUNK'D GUY

2. Who's the _____ from the
       BLOND CHICK WITH THE FLAT NOSE

_____ who divorced that
SEXY AL PACINO MOVIE WITH THE SONG

_____ and sold all his jewelry?
RICH COSMETICS BALD GUY

3. Who's the _____ who started out as the
       BUSTED ACTRESS

youngest kid to win an Oscar for her role in that

_____ that co-starred her
DADDY–DAUGHTER CON MAN MOVIE

_____ who married the _____ and
REAL DAD   ANGEL WITH THE HAIR

she—the kid—married the _____
TENNIS PLAYER WITH THE TANTRUMS

and everybody got divorced?

4. Who's the _____ who used to be married to
EGOCENTRIC GUY

_____ and started the whole cable news thing with that
BARBARELLA

_____ in the _____ in that _____
STATION   CITY THAT GOT BURNED TO THE GROUND   MOVIE

where the _____ gives the _____
CHARACTER WITH THE MUSTACHE   TARA LADY

that _____?
CLASSIC BREAK-UP LINE

5. Who's that _____ whose
ACTOR WITH ALL THE LESS-FAMOUS BROTHERS

_____ was in that _____ and they got divorced
RECLUSIVE WIFE   NOIR MOVIE

and he left his _____ that
DAUGHTER WHO'S NAMED AFTER A COUNTRY

horrible message on her answering machine and in the

meantime he's in that _____ with
COMEDY SHOW ABOUT A COMEDY SHOW

that _____ and imitates the _____
FUNNY WOMAN WHO WEARS GLASSES   HOCKEY

____ and wrote that _____?
MOM   MOVIE ABOUT THE HIGH SCHOOL CLIQUES

6. Who's that _____ from the _____ whose first name
BLOND GUY   BOY BAND

is the same as that _____ who had cancer and dated that
BICYCLIST

_____ who also had cancer?
OLDER BUT COOL SINGER

7. Who are those _____, one of whom wasn't eaten
TWO VEGAS GUYS

by a tiger but, unfortunately, the _____ was?
OTHER ONE

Strangely Named Celebrity Offspring

8. Who's the _____
ONE WE'LL ALWAYS THINK OF AS THE OFFICIAL TRUMP
_____ who gave her _____ practically the same
WOMAN   DAUGHTER
name while her _____ with _____ gave his ___ some
TACKY EX   WIFE #3   SON
fake-royal-sounding name?

9. Who's the _____ who named her ____ a
AUSTRALIAN ACTRESS   BABY
day of the week she wasn't born on?

10. Who's the _____ who stole _____
SUPERSTAR WITH ALL THE KIDS   WHAT'S-
_____ superstar _____ and gave their ____
HER-NAME'S   HUSBAND   FIRST
_____ the same name as that dog in the clas-
BIOLOGICAL CHILD
sic children's book?

11. Who's the _____
AMERICAN BLONDE WHO'S ALWAYS USING A BRITISH
_____ who was the girlfriend of the ____ in that ____
ACCENT   BARD   MOVIE
and then she named her real-life _____ after a fruit?
DAUGHTER

12. Who's the _____ who dangled
SINGER WITH THE MISSING NOSE
one of his kids from the balcony and calls two out of
three of them the _____ as the _____?
SAME NAME   PURPLE RAIN GUY

13. Who's the _____ who was naked and pregnant on
ACTRESS

that _____ cover who named her __ exactly what
MAGAZINE   KID

that magazine is famous for?

14. Who was the _____ who gave his Valley Girl
ZANY ROCKER

daughter that sort of _____?
OUTER SPACE NAME

15. Who's that _____ who became a Stepford Wife
SWEET ACTRESS

when she married the _____ and their ____
COUCH JUMPER   BABY

_____ sounds like that thing with the fringe
DAUGHTER'S NAME

on top from that _____ where the
MUSICAL ABOUT THE STATE

_____ is as high as that _____ eye?
VEGETABLE   BIG GRAY ANIMAL'S

16. Who's the _____ who married the
BLONDE TO END ALL BLONDES

_____ who's in the _____ by the _____
BASEBALL PLAYER   SONG   "TROUBLED WATER"

_____ before she married the _____ who wrote that
GUYS   BROOKLYNITE

_____ and
DEPRESSING PLAY ABOUT THE MAN WHO SCHLEPS THE SUITCASES

sang "Happy Birthday" to the _____
PRESIDENT SHE MAYBE SLEPT

_____, and maybe his _____, too?
WITH   BROTHER

17. Who's the _____ with that _____
GERMAN SUPERMODEL   DESIGNER REALITY

_____ who married the _____
SHOW   SINGER WITH THE SCARS THAT LOOK TRIBAL

_____ and his name is the same as those poor baby
BUT AREN'T

animals that get clubbed that _____
WHAT'S-HER-FACE WITH THE LEG

was trying to save, unlike her marriage to the _____?
BEATLE

18. Who's the _____ famous _____ who
FAMOUS BLONDE'S   BLOND DAUGHTER

hooked up with the _____ who tried
FUNNY BLOND GUY WITH THE NOSE

to commit suicide, which wasn't very funny, but neither

was that _____?
MOVIE THEY DID TOGETHER

19. Who's that _____
BLOND ACTRESS WHOSE LIPS LOOK LIKE SHE JUST ATE A

_____ who married the _____ for
LEMON   "YOU HAD ME FROM HELLO" SINGER

about 10 minutes and was in that _____ about
ROMANTIC COMEDY

the pudgy secretary with that _____ who
GRINNING ENGLISH ACTOR

stopped grinning when he got caught doing things in his

car that he had to apologize for on national TV?

20. Who's the _____ whose _____

ACTOR WITH THE CLEFT CHIN   SON WITH THE CLEFT

____ got to marry that _____

CHIN   MUCH YOUNGER WELSH ACTRESS WITH THE

_____ who starred in that _____ about the women

THREE NAMES   MUSICAL

in jail in sexy costumes?

21. Who's the '80s _____ with the _____

                    SINGER DAD   REALLY SKINNY BLOND

_____ who had a baby after she got famous on that

DAUGHTER

_____ with the other _____

REALITY SHOW   SKINNY BLONDE WHO GOT REALLY

_____, but no one knows exactly what for?

FAMOUS

22. Who's the _____

                    EXILED LEADER WITH THE NAME THAT SOUNDS LIKE THOSE

_____ who comes from the _____

SHAGGY, MATTED ANIMALS   COUNTRY WITH

_____ that the _____ always gives speeches

THE MONKS   PRETTY WOMAN GUY

about?

23. Who's that _____ everyone remembers for

                    OUTRAGEOUS COMEDIAN

that wrestling scene in his ____ whose real name is the

                            MOVIE

same as that _____ except for the middle?

                FIGURE SKATER'S

★ **Take 10** ★

Flaming Redheads

Who's—

1. The _____?
   HARRY POTTER FAMILY THAT SOUNDS LIKE A BUNCH OF WEASELS

2. The _____
   FUNNY, NEUROTIC, JEWISH NEW YORK FILMMAKER WHOSE

   _____?
   PROBLEMS WE WON'T GO INTO HERE

3. One of those _____?
   HOUSEWIVES

4. The _____?
   CSI: MIAMI GUY

5. The _____?
   ONE WITH BEAUTIFUL FLOWING HAIR WITH THE GAY ROOMMATE

6. _____?
   RAGGEDY ANDY'S SISTER

7. The _____?
   FUNNY ONE MARRIED TO RICKY

8. The _____?
   ONE WHO TUGGED HER EAR AT THE END OF HER SHOW

9. The _____?
   HAMBURGER CLOWN

10. The _____?
    PIGTAILED HAMBURGER GIRL

★ **Take 10** ★

Guys in White Suits

Who's—

1. The _____?
CHICKEN GUY

2. The _____?
ISLAND GUY WITH THE ACCENT EVERYONE IMITATED

3. The _____?
ISLAND GUY'S SIDEKICK

4. The _____?
PRETENTIOUS JOURNALIST

5. The _____?
"HI-YO, SILVER" GUY

6. The _____?
DISCO GUY

7. The _____?
GUY WITH THE ARROW THROUGH HIS HEAD

8. The _____?
GUY WITH THE ICE CREAM TRUCK

9. The _____?
WRITER YOU ALWAYS PICTURE ON A STEAMBOAT

10. The _____?
BAD GUY IN THE CAVE

★ Take 10 ★

Guys with Mustaches

Who's—

1. The _____?
PRESIDENT WHO CHARGED UP THE HILL

2. The _____?
CRAZY SPANISH ARTIST WITH THE DROOPY CLOCKS

3. The _____?
FUNNY GUY WITH THE BROTHERS AND THE CIGAR

4. The _____?
RELATIVITY GUY

5. The _____?
SIMPSONS' NEIGHBOR

6. The _____?
GUY FROM COLOMBIA WHO MADE COFFEE

7. The _____?
BAD GERMAN

8. The _____?
BAD IRAQI

9. The _____?
BAD CUBAN (WITH A BEARD, TOO)

10. The _____?
SILENT FILM GUY

Can't Stop the Beat

★ Tongue Tipper ★

1. Who's that _____ who was married to the ___
SONGBIRD   OLD
_____ whose name sounds like the _____
PRODUCER   RAZR PHONE
_____, who made her a superstar, then she had a
COMPANY
breakdown, a divorce, a _____, a comeback, another
BAD MOVIE
marriage, and more hits than the _____?
GUY ON THE STAMP

2. Who are those _____ with the ___ who
MEXICAN GUYS   HATS
serenade you in restaurants whether you want them

to or not and then you need another one of those

_____?
DRINKS WITH THE SALT

3. What's that _____ with the _____
SWEDISH SINGING GROUP   MUSICAL
that became a movie with the _____
ACTRESS WITH THE

_____ and the _____ and
ACCENTS   007 GUY WHO'S ALWAYS IN ADS FOR WATCHES

there's that big ____ based on how you say "Help!" when
              SONG

your ship is going down?

4. Who's that _____ who always wore big red
              MALE BRITISH SINGER

lipstick who isn't the other _____
                              BRITISH SINGER WHO HAD SEX IN

_____, just like that _____ from the _____
BATHROOMS   FOOT-TAPPING SENATOR   POTATO

____ probably did?
STATE

5. Who's the _____ even though she's
              SUPERMODEL WHO STILL LOOKS 30

over 50, and the _____ who wrote a _____ and
              EX-HUSBAND   SONG ABOUT HER

ran into a tree and _____ who slept with some teen,
                    ANOTHER ONE

and so much for being a supermodel with your pick of guys?

6. Who are those _____
              TWO DITZY SINGING (OR AT LEAST LIP-SYNCHING)

_____ with the same last name as the _____
SISTERS   GUY WHO WAS STILL

_____ till he went to prison for
LOOKING FOR HIS WIFE'S MURDERER
something else?

7. Who's the _____ with that _____
              ONE-HIT WONDER DAD   SONG WITH THE SILLY

____ who was on the _____
NAME   DANCING SHOW WITH OTHER B-LISTERS

while his _____ hit the big-time with her _____
          DAUGHTER   TEENY-BOPPER

_____ and tour and those racy pictures by that _____
TV SHOW   SUPERSTAR

_____ who always gets people to take off their
PHOTOGRAPHER

clothes?

8. Who's the _____ who's from that _____
GUY WITH THE DREADS   CARIBBEAN

_____ who made that ____ that is part
PLACE WITH THE JERK CHICKEN   MUSIC

of his _____ famous all over the world and now there's a
RELIGION

_____?
BOOK AND MOVIE ABOUT A DOG WITH HIS NAME

9. What's that _____ that's sort of based on the
TEEN TV MUSICAL

same _____ that Leonard Bernstein
TEEN SHAKESPEAREAN TRAGEDY

made into that _____
BROADWAY SHOW WITH THE DANCING STREET GANGS

but the TV one is the only one that has a happy ending

because the _____ produced it?
MOUSE HOUSE

10. Who were those two avant-garde dancers and the _____
ONE WHO

_____ whose name sounds like that
DIED BECAUSE OF HER SCARF

_____ and the _____ who sounds like that
DOUGHNUT PLACE   OTHER ONE

_____ you use to make s'mores?
COOKIE

11. Who's that _____ whose name sounds just like that
MARGARITA GUY

_____ investment god who always eats lunch at the
BILLIONAIRE

same diner in that _____ where the steaks-by-mail
MIDWESTERN CITY

come from that you always see advertised in that _____
HIGHBROW

_____ people only subscribe to for the cartoons?
MAGAZINE

12. What's that _____ with the _____ that
DICTATOR MUSICAL   CRYING SONG

_____ did everything but kill to get the lead part
WHAT'S-HER-FACE

in and co-starred that _____?
MASK OF ZORRO GUY

13. What's that _____ with that _____ that
CITY DOWN SOUTH   HOKEY RADIO SHOW

the _____ is on a lot and so is that _____
AMERICAN IDOL WINNER   TINY SINGER

_____ and the _____ and the
WITH THE HAIR AND THE BOOBS   AMUSEMENT PARK

city became a movie directed by the _____?
NO-PLOT GUY

14. What's that _____ on
WAKE-UP SONG THEY PLAY IN THE ARMY AND CAMP

that _____ that they turned into a _____
ANNOYING INSTRUMENT   SALTY CORN

_____ you see in vending machines right next to that other
SNACK

_____?
SALTY SNACK THAT TURNS YOUR FINGERS ORANGE

15. Who's the _____ at that _____ where
ONE WHO WAS IGNORED   AWARDS SHOW

the _____ kissed, even though she was kissed, too?
OTHER TWO

16. What's that _____ that _____
POLKA INSTRUMENT EVERYONE HATES   WHAT'S-HIS-

_____ used to play?
NAME WITH THE BUBBLES

★ SOUND ALIKES II ★

Fill in the blanks with words that sound alike, more or less.
Sometimes less.

1. Cheap cocaine:

_____

Cramp in the neck:

_____

Piece of earthenware:

_____

What people who die do:

_____

2. Sport where players don't have a lot of teeth:

_____

What you play when you don't go to school:

_____

Someone who's very religious and an old sock:

_____

What Cindy Crawford's cheek is:

_____

3. Manning quarterback who isn't Eli:

_____

Russian president who flexes his muscles:

_____

What you're doin' when you're on the green with a golf club:

_____

Silly stuff that comes in a plastic egg:

_____

4. The beginning of a thousand boring kids' jokes:

_____

Thing you clutter a shelf with:

_____

Chocolate-covered candy bar that sounds like a pet:

_____

1.9-calorie mint in tiny plastic box:

_____

5. Girl who lived at the Plaza:

_____

Lady who gave household hints:

_____

Things you put ornaments and tangled lights on during holidays:

_____

Bad thing you get from ticks:

_____

6. Underwater bomb:

_____

City in Ohio that doesn't start with a "C":

_____

Small insect that makes you itch:

_____

Triangular chip from Lay's:

_____

7. Feminist magazine:

_____

Long-running musical about the French Revolution (abbrev.):

_____

Natural childbirth technique:

_____

Wooly animals in the Andes:

_____

8. Potato chip with ridges:

_____

Guns for hunting deer:

_____

Expensive mushrooms pigs find:

_____

Insignificant items:

_____

9. World of scholars, or at least professors:

_____

Nut everyone brings you back from Hawaii, as if you can't get them everywhere else:

_____

Noodles with bright orange cheese:

_____

Chewy coconut cookie:

_____

History the Way We Remember It

★ Tongue Tipper ★

1. Who's the _____ who lived in
GUY WITH THE KITE AND THE KEY

the ___ with the ___ but was born in the _____
CITY   BELL   CITY WITH

_____ where the _____ told every-
THE TEA PARTY   GUY WITH THE HORSE

one, "_____"?
SOMEONE'S COMING! SOMEONE'S COMING!

2. Who was the _____ with the
PRESIDENT IN THE WHEELCHAIR

_____ who declared _____ when the
STRONG, TOOTHY WIFE   THAT WAR

_____ in the _____ got bombed
HARBOR   STATE WITH THE GRASS SKIRTS

by the _____?
KAMIKAZE GUYS

3. What was that _____ of the guy who talked
PORNO NAME

to those _____ in the garage about that
TWO REPORTERS

_____ and made them so famous that
HISTORIC BREAK-IN

in the movie one was played by the _____ and
SUNDANCE GUY

the other one got _____ to be him?
RAIN MAN

4. Who's the _____ that looks like the _____ who
GENERAL   FRIED CHICKEN GUY

battled that _____ whose name sounds like a swear
INDIAN CHIEF

word at that _____ that isn't the _____
BIG LITTLE PLACE   OTHER INDIAN PLACE

where someone wanted his heart to be buried?

5. What's that _____ that was popular at those _____
FLAPPER DANCE   ILLEGAL

____ everybody went to during that _____
BARS   TIME WHEN YOU WEREN'T

_____ and it ended with that ___ when rich
ALLOWED TO DRINK   ERA

people lost all of their money and jumped off buildings or

became one of those _____ who rode trains and carried
PEOPLE

their clothing on sticks?

6. Who were the ___ and ___ who were both president
DAD   SON

before, oy, the _____?
OTHER TWO

7. Who's the _____ who started the whole
BACK OF THE BUS LADY

_____ that led to the _____ at that _____ that's
MOVEMENT   BIG SPEECH   PLACE IN DC

on the ___?
COIN

8. Who's that ___ who flew solo across the Atlantic and
PILOT

inspired that _____ whose plane got lost above that
LADY PILOT

_____ that guys wear with
<u>TRIANGLE THAT SOUNDS LIKE THE SHORTS</u>

those _____?
<u>TACKY, COLORFUL SHIRTS</u>

9. Who's that _____ with the name everyone yells when they
<u>INDIAN</u>

jump off a cliff and that _____ is named for his
<u>MOVIE IN NEW YORK</u>

tribe and starred the _____?
<u>SALAD DRESSING GUY WHO DIED</u>

10. Who's the ___ that became an insurance company and
<u>GUY</u>

we're always asked to write our version of his name some-

where because he was the first to sign that _____
<u>IMPORTANT PAPER</u>

on the _____?
<u>HOLIDAY WITH THE FIREWORKS</u>

11. What's that _____ that's the same number as the
<u>AMENDMENT</u>

_____ and politicians plead it a lot and say it's
<u>FRENCH PERFUME</u>

their right because it's part of that ___?
<u>BILL</u>

12. What's the _____ in New York that's a type of pencil
<u>FAMOUS FORT</u>

and it was captured in 1775 by the _____
<u>GUY WHO TURNED OUT TO BE</u>

_____ and the _____?
<u>A TRAITOR</u>   <u>COLONEL WHO TURNED INTO A FURNITURE STORE</u>

13. What's that _____ that you see
<u>PINK BIRD THAT'S SOMETIMES PLASTIC</u>

on the license plates for the _____ where
<u>STATE WITH THE OLD PEOPLE</u>

_____ lost the election before he made that
<u>WHAT'S-HIS-NAME</u>

_____ about pollution that got him that ___?
<u>POWERPOINT MOVIE</u>   <u>PRIZE</u>

14. Who are those two presidents who once ran on the same

ticket—and the _____ told the _____
ONE WHO WAS PRESIDENT FIRST   RUSSIAN

___ to _____ and the _____ kept telling us to
GUY   DO SOMETHING   SECOND ONE

_____?
DO SOMETHING WITH HIS MOUTH

15. Who's the _____ who wrote about the ____ and the other
HARRIET   CABIN

_____ who worked on that _____
CIVIL WAR HARRIET   UNDERCOVER THING THAT'S

_____ until _____ made that ___
LIKE A TRAIN   WHAT'S-HIS-NAME WITH THE BEARD   BIG

_____?
PROCLAMATION

16. Who are those _____
OLD NORDIC WARRIORS WITH THE HORNS ON THEIR

_____ that became a football team in that ____ where the
HELMETS   STATE

_____ ran for the Senate?
SNL LIBERAL

17. Who's the _____ when he came
ITALIAN GUY WHO FOUND AMERICA

over on those _____ and then the _____
THREE SHIPS   PEOPLE WHO WORE

_____ came over on their ____ and
THE SHOES WITH THE BUCKLES   SHIP

landed on that _____?
ROCK THAT USED TO BE A CAR

18. Who's that _____ who drank that
ANCIENT GREEK PHILOSOPHER

_____ that sounds like that _____ you do when some-
POISON   MANEUVER

one's choking?

19. Who's that medieval ___ who presided over that ___
                              KING   TABLE

with all the knights that they made into that _____
                                                       MUSICAL

with Richard Burton and the ___ who played _____
                                   GUY   SIR WHAT'S-

_____, who was in all those commercials for Emerald
HIS-NAME

Nuts before he died?

20. What's that _____ where everyone
                PART OF RUSSIA THAT'S REALLY COLD

was exiled, like that _____ back
                   GULAG WRITER WITH THE LONG NAME

when it was Communist and had all those statues of the

___ whose name sounds like the _____?
GUY   BEATLE

21. What's the romantic _____ that sounds like the ter-
                          CUBAN SONG

rible _____ that isn't the other awful _____ with
     CUBAN PRISON   ONE IN IRAQ

the controversial _____ that sounds like it should be a
                 TORTURE

sport you'd do in Hawaii but definitely isn't?

22. Who's that _____ who became a pastry that's
              SHORT FRENCH GENERAL

always in the same bakery case as that _____
                               COFFEE-FLAVORED, LIQUOR-

_____ made with that _____ that
SOAKED ITALIAN DESSERT   SPECIAL CHEESE

sounds a little like that 1920s _____
                           GANGSTER WHO THEY FINALLY GOT ON

_____?
TAX EVASION

23. What's that _____ that took up a whole shelf and
            ENCYCLOPEDIA

sounded like that _____ with the _____ who
                  COUNTRY   PRINCE WITH THE EARS

was married to the _____ and the _____
PRINCESS WHO DIED   SINGER WITH THE

_____ sang that _____ about her that was really another
GLASSES   SONG

song first and he just changed the lyrics?

24. What's that _____ they used to send messages in
TAPPING CODE

wartime, unless they were using those _____ like the
DIRTY BIRDS

ones Burt Lancaster loved in that _____?
PRISON MOVIE

25. Who's the _____ and dated that _____
GUY WHO RULED ROME   BEAUTIFUL

_____ before he was stabbed by the _____ and now
EGYPTIAN   "ET TU" GUY

he's a salad made with those _____ most people want it
SALTY FISH

without?

★ Take 10 ★

Famous Generals

Who's—

1. The _____?
   GEORGE C. SCOTT ONE

2. The _____?
   ONE THAT MAKES CHEERIOS

3. The _____?
   ONE THAT'S A COMPANY THAT BROUGHT *GOOD* THINGS TO LIFE

4. The _____?
   ONE WHO SAID HE'D RETURN

5. The _____
   ONE THAT WAS THE WORLD'S BIGGEST CAR MAKER UNTIL IT

   _____?
   WASN'T ANYMORE

6. The _____
   ONE THAT BECAME A PRESIDENT EVERYONE USED TO SAY THEY

   _____?
   LIKED BECAUSE OF HIS FIRST NAME

7. The _____?
   ONE THAT'S A SOAP OPERA

8. The _____
   ONE THAT'S AN OLD-FASHIONED PLACE WHERE FOLKS WOULD BUY

   _____?
   GINGHAM, FLOUR, AND SASPARILLA

9. The _____?
   ONE THAT'S A TICKET

10. The _____
    ONE WHO IS ON EVERY CIGARETTE PACKAGE

★ **Take 10** ★

Presidential Losers

Who's—

1. The _____ who married the _____?
   SWIFT BOAT GUY   KETCHUP LADY

2. The _____ who was a guy, with maybe an extra baby?
   BRECK GIRL

3. The _____, despite the headline?
   ONE TRUMAN BEAT

4. The _____?
   WOMAN

5. The _____?
   ONE WHO EVERYONE THINKS REALLY WON

6. The _____?
   E.D. GUY

7. The _____ and the _____?
   SHORT GUY WITH THE HELMET   SO-SO FAMOUS SISTER

8. The _____?
   GUY WITH THE EARS, PIE CHARTS, AND BILLIONS

9. The _____?
   SHRIEKER

10. _____?
    MR. 9/11

Animal Planet

★ Tongue Tipper ★

1. What's that _____ that sounds like a
        REALLY HEAVY LIZARD

_____ and is mean, not like the _____
JAPANESE ROBE   MAGIC ONE

those _____ couldn't stop singing about
        THREE FOLK SINGERS

for decades, just like the _____ and the
                            ONE ABOUT THE TOOL

_____?
GUY WITH THE BOAT

2. Who's the _____ that's not the _____
              LOVELY SPIDER   KIND THAT BITES

_____ who saved the life of that _____
HER MATE'S HEAD OFF   LITTLE

___ in the _____ by the _____, just like the old
PIG   CLASSIC   ESSAY GUY

farmer did with _his_ little pig in the _____ that was
                                          MOVIE

nominated for an Academy Award?

3. What's that _____ that sounds like the wormy
          TRACTOR COMPANY

insect in that _____ that com-
                KIDS BOOK WITH THE HOLES IN THE PAGES

petes with the _____ that sounds like the
                OTHER TRACTOR COMPANY

_____?
ANIMAL WITH THE TICKS

4. Who's that _____—not _____—who lived in
                 WOMAN   TARZAN'S GIRLFRIEND

the jungle with all those _____ like the one who
                          HUMANLIKE ANIMALS

co-starred in that _____ with the _____?
                   MOVIE   GIPPER PRESIDENT

5. What's that _____ that eats the _____
                  CUDDLY AUSTRALIAN ANIMAL   PLANT

_____ just like that other _____
THAT'S IN COUGH DROPS   FLAVOR THEY PUT IN

_____ that feels cool in your throat, which is why
COUGH DROPS

they put it in some cigarettes, like the _____
                                          BRAND THAT SOUNDS

_____?
LIKE THE TOWN WHERE THEY PUT THE WITCHES ON TRIAL

6. What's that _____ that's
                  CLASSIC AMERICAN CAR THAT'S A WILD HORSE

not the _____
        ONE THAT KEPT CATCHING ON FIRE IN THE '60s AND SOUNDS

_____ and was exposed by the _____
LIKE A BEAN   CRUSADER-TURNED-JERK

who's always running for president?

7. What's that _____
                  KIND OF CAT WITH THE SMUSHED-IN FACE THAT SOUNDS

_____ that decorators have if they don't have
LIKE AN ORIENTAL RUG

one of those _____ that sounds like
             DOGS WITH THE SMUSHED-IN FACE

the _____?
    OLD NAME FOR BEIJING

8. What's the _____ that lives in
HUGE, UGLY BUT KIND OF CUTE MAMMAL

mud and water that everyone confuses with the _____
HUGE, UGLY-

_____ that sounds like the _____
UGLY MAMMAL WITH THE HORNS   REAL NAME

_____?
FOR A NOSE JOB

9. What's that _____ that lives in the lake who's about as
MONSTER

believable as that _____ with the prints in the snow who
HAIRY GUY

has that _____ that sort of sounds like the
OTHER OFFICIAL NAME

_____ of that _____ with the gravelly voice?
NICKNAME   TRUMPET PLAYER

10. What's that kind of ___ they massage in Japan with the
COW

same name as that_____ on the ___ that used
BASKETBALL PLAYER   TEAM

to have that _____
GUY WHO CHANGED HIS NAME WHEN HE CONVERTED TO

_____ and that _____
ISLAM   RETIRED PLAYER WHO WENT PUBLIC WITH HIS

___ and became more beloved than ever?
HIV

11. What are those _____ that people
FISH THAT AREN'T GOLDFISH

get that are blue or red and they sell for like $3 at pet

shops, not far from those _____
FAKE BONES THAT ARE SUPPOSED TO

_____ and that _____ Ed McMahon
CLEAN DOGS' TEETH   CLASSIC DOG FOOD

used to advertise when he wasn't harping about that

_____?
CONTEST THAT CAME IN THE MAIL

★ SOUND ALIKES III ★

Fill in the blanks with words that sound alike, more or less. Sometimes less.

1. Guy who led rats and kids out of Hamelin:

_____

Guy who picked a peck of pickled peppers:

_____

Real name of Spider-Man:

_____

Husband who put wife in a pumpkin shell:

_____

2. First name of scared cartoon dog:

_____

Famous board game with words:

_____

What you do when you write down something quickly:

_____

Native American guy kids always learn about at Thanksgiving:

_____

3. Someone who sells love:

_____

Someone who breaks into computers:

_____

Someone with a backpack on a trail:

_____

Annoying drunk at a comedy club:

_____

4. Red gems:

_____

Disease you can get if bitten by a squirrel:

_____

Jewish leaders:

_____

Type of steaks:

_____

5. Utah religion:

_____

Famous singing Ethel:

_____

Part lady, part fish:

_____

Lady who gives you a parking ticket:

_____

6. Round thing on the moon:

_____

Cute word for a rodent:

_____

Author of _Jurassic Park_:

_____

Old bread you put on a salad:

_____

7. Yellow rubber toy that's fun in the tub:

_____

Hard rubber hockey disc:

_____

What you do when your head is in the toilet:

_____

School with acquitted soccer players, NCAA powerhouse:

_____

8. First Lady that's an ice cream (first name only):

_____

Bird who wants a cracker:

_____

Little Richard's Miss:

_____

What you deck the halls with:

_____

9. Person with an online diary no one really wants to read:

_____

Someone who runs as a form of exercise:

_____

Person who throws bowling pins or sticks on fire in the air:

_____

Someone who brings illegal stuff across state lines:

_____

Page-Turners

★ Tongue Tipper ★

1. What's that _____
BOOK ABOUT GOING OFF TO LIVE BY YOURSELF

_____ that was written by that _____
ON A POND   EARLY AMERICAN

___ who was friends with the other _____
GUY   EARLY AMERICAN

_____ whose middle name is like that
GUY WITH THREE NAMES

cartoon character you have to find in that _____?
                                            KIDS' BOOK

2. What's that _____
BOOK THAT'S ALWAYS AT THE AIRPORT ABOUT

_____, like the time that
GETTING OUT OF HORRIBLE SITUATIONS

_____—not the _____—
AUSTRALIAN   "SHRIMP ON THE BARBIE" ACTOR

the other one, with the _____, got attacked
                        TV NATURE SHOW

by the fish and died?

3. Who's the _____ who wrote the
GUY WHOSE FIRST NAME IS A STATE

_____ that's set in the ___
PLAY WHERE MARLON BRANDO YELLED "STELLA"   CITY

with the _____ and the _____ and the
HURRICANE   AGENCY THAT SCREWED UP

_____ that's like that carnival with all the
PARADE WITH ALL THE BEADS

feathers in that _____?
SEXY SOUTH AMERICAN CITY

4. What's that _____ they used to get the _____
WEAPON   WHALE IN THE BOOK

and the _____ but you would never use on
SHARK IN THE MOVIE

those _____ that are always getting killed
BIG, SLOW COW CREATURES

by boat propellers and the other _____ people
SMARTER ONES

swim with that look like they're smiling?

5. Who's the _____ who goes down the ___ with the
BOY ON THE RAFT   RIVER

____ in that famous book that isn't the one about the ___
SLAVE   BOY

_____, but both were written by that ___ with the
WITH THE FENCE   GUY

same last name as the _____?
PRETTY COUNTRY SINGER

6. What's the ___ in that poem by the _____ who
BIRD   MORBID GUY

lived in that _____ with the _____
CITY NEAR DC   BASEBALL TEAM THAT'S

_____?
ANOTHER BIRD

7. What's that _____ that turned out to be a total lie by
MEMOIR

the _____ that _____ loved and she forgave on
AUTHOR   WHAT'S-HER-NAME

that _____, but then she
 TALK SHOW WITH THE OLD GUY IN SUSPENDERS

changed her mind and now there's no way she's giving him

one of those ____ she gives everyone else?
 CARS

8. Who's the _____ who wrote all those mysteries,
 ENGLISH LADY

like the _____ with that _____, and
 ONE ON THE TRAIN   BELGIAN DETECTIVE

whenever you play that _____ with the knife in the
 BOARD GAME

conservatory and the gun in the billiard room and that

_____, it feels like you're in one
 COLONEL WHOSE NAME IS A CONDIMENT

of her books?

9. What's that one-panel _____
 COMIC STRIP WITH THE TALKING COWS

whose _____ decided to quit, even though everyone had
 AUTHOR

his calendars and mugs all over the place, unlike the ___
 GUY

with the _____ or the _____
 CUBICLE COMIC STRIP   GUY MARRIED TO JANE PAULEY

with his _____ who keep plugging away?
 COMIC STRIP

10. What's that _____ the _____ in the poem wore around
 BIG BIRD   OLD GUY

his neck that made him feel almost as bad as the _____ in
 WOMAN

the ____ with the _____ on her chest?
 BOOK   LETTER

11. Who's the _____ who said
 AMERICAN POET WITH THE WINTERY NAME

something about _____ that inspired the title of
 WHAT ROAD TO TAKE

the _____ that's not by the _____ whose
    SPIRITUAL BESTSELLER   INDIAN GUY

last name sounds like that _____?
                      SLIMY VEGETABLE YOU PUT IN GUMBO

12. Who's the _____ like
       GUY WHO WRITES ALL THOSE TECHNO-THRILLERS

the _____ and even when you're reading
   ONE ABOUT THE SUBMARINE

them you either see that _____ in the starring
                OLD JAMES BOND GUY

role, or you see the _____?
         INDIANA JONES GUY

13. What's the _____ that sort of
     CLASSIC GIRLS' BOOK ABOUT LIFE OUT WEST

sounds like that weekly _____
          NPR SHOW THAT WAS MADE INTO A MOVIE

with that _____ who always talks about
    TALL GUY FROM MINNESOTA

the news from _____?
     SOMEPLACE SAD

★ Take 10 ★

Poets from A to Z

Who's—

1. The _____?
   HEAD-IN-THE-OVEN LADY

2. The _____?
   WIFE OF BATH GUY

3. The _____?
   ONE WHO STAYED IN HER ROOM

4. The _____?
   WASTELAND ONE

5. the _____?
   lowercase guy

6. The _____?
   CAGED BIRD LADY

7. The _____?
   ONE ON RADIO WITH THE BOWTIE EVEN THOUGH YOU CAN'T SEE IT

8. The _____?
   LEAVES OF GRASS MAN

9. The _____?
   JEWISH BEATNIK

10. The _____
    GUYS-DON'T-MAKE-PASSES-AT-GIRLS-WHO-WEAR-GLASSES
    _____?
    ROUND TABLE LADY

★ Take 10 ★

Magazines, Etc.

What's—

1. The _____?
   ONE WITH THE SWIMSUITS

2. The _____
   ONE WITH THE WREATHS MADE OUT OF HAND-LOOMED LACE AND
   _____?
   BABY PINECONES

3. The _____?
   ONE THAT GETS FIRST CRACK AT BRANGELINA STORIES

4. The _____?
   ONE THAT GETS SECOND CRACK

5. The _____?
   ONE THAT SHOWS YOU HOW OUT OF STYLE YOU ARE

6. The _____?
   ONE THAT LISTS THE RICH GUYS

7. The _____?
   GIRLS' MAGAZINE GIRLS DON'T READ ONCE THEY'RE THAT AGE

8. The _____?
   SMALL ONE FOR COUCH POTATOES

9. The _____?
   SMALL ONE THAT'S AS OLD AS ITS JOKES

10. The _____?
    ONE ABOUT THE WORLD THAT YOU ALWAYS FIND IN STACKS AT
    _____?
    GARAGE SALES

What's in Store

★ Tongue Tipper ★

1. What's that _____
   STORE WITH THE BRAS AND THE SOFT-CORE

   _____ with all the models from that _____
   FASHION SHOW   SOUTH

   _____ that's also a kind of nut you find
   AMERICAN COUNTRY

   in those cans of mixed nuts made by that _____
                                            COMPANY

   whose _____ is always wearing a top hat?
          MASCOT

2. What's that convenience store with the _____
                                              TWO NUMBERS

   that's always getting robbed and sells those _____
                                                 GIANT SODA

   ____ and _____ that sound like what you do
   CUPS   FROZEN DRINKS

   when you drink them?

3. Who's the ____ whose last name is the same as the ____ that
ACTOR   STORE

sponsors the Thanksgiving parade on the street where the

miracle was in that _____ that's on every Christmas, just
OLD MOVIE

like that _____ with _____ on the bridge?
OTHER CLASSIC   WHAT'S-HIS-NAME

4. What's that _____ that's a classier
BIG STORE WITH THE RED CIRCLES

version of the _____ and the
BIG STORE WITH THE BLUE-LIGHT SPECIALS

other ____ with the famous catalog and the Kenmore
STORE

appliances and the ____ you buy for Father's Day?
TOOLS

5. What's the _____ that used to say to the world,
BRAND OF BIG CAR

"I've made it!" but now says, "I'm old!"—except for its ___
SUV

_____ which says, "I'm guzzling gas!"—and now hip peo-
VERSION

ple buy those _____, like that _____
CARS THAT USE BATTERIES   SUPERPOPULAR

_____, and then they go shopping at that ____ with the
TOYOTA   STORE

organic raspberries that cost $17 a pound?

6. What's that _____ in Maine that has almost
OUTDOORSY CATALOG

the same name as the _____ and is like the ____
VETERAN RAPPER   OTHER

_____ that sounds like it's at the end of the world?
OUTDOORSY CATALOG

7. What's that _____ with all the hammers and light-
ORANGE STORE

ing fixtures that's put most mom-and-pop stores out of

business, just like that _____ with the
HUMONGOUS SUPERMARKET

20-pound jars of mayonnaise and plastic platters of sushi,

and the _____ started by that
EVERYTHING STORE WITH THE SMILEY FACE

_____ with the same last name as that _____
FOLKSY BILLIONAIRE   FOLKSY TV

_____ who couldn't stop saying "good night" to each other?
FAMILY

8. What's that _____ that
HANGING THING YOU RELAX IN UNTIL YOU FALL OUT

sounds like the first half of that _____ that
HIGH-END GADGET STORE

was as overpriced as that _____ with the
DALLAS DEPARTMENT STORE

Christmas catalog with stuff like gem-encrusted golf club

covers?

9. What's that _____ that's the same
BOOKSTORE THAT'S ON THE COMPUTER

name as that river with those _____ if the
FISH THAT EAT PEOPLE

_____ they used to use in medicine don't get
BLOODSUCKING WORMS

them first?

10. What's that _____ with the
FAMOUS OLD GROCERY STORE CHAIN'S NAME

letters that sound like those _____ high school kids take to
TESTS

show how smart they are in certain subjects and maybe

get accepted at places like that _____,
FANCY COLLEGE THAT'S A COLOR

or that _____ that sounds like that _____
WOMEN'S COLLEGE   SNIPES ACTOR

and graduated Hillary?

11. What's that _____ with the parakeets
DEFUNCT FIVE-AND-DIME STORE

and candy that went under that sounded like that _____
LIQUID YOU

_____?
WASH YOUR SWEATERS IN

12. What's the _____ with the _____ and the _____
JEWELRY STORE   MOVIE   HAUNTING

_____ that starred the _____
SONG   CLASSY ACTRESS WITH THE CIGARETTE

_____ that was first a book by the ___ Philip Seymour
HOLDER   GUY

Hoffman played in the movie about his other _____
FAR LESS

_____?
CHARMING BOOK

★ SOUND ALIKES IV ★

Fill in the blanks with words that sound alike, more or less. Sometimes less.

1. Sound of little feet:

_____

Crazy guy in *Wonderland*:

_____

Batter who can hit from both sides of the plate; also a bisexual:

_____

Someone who watches your kid when you're away:

_____

2. What you say when a tree is falling:

_____

Guy who brought sexy back (surname):

_____

Rapper/record producer:

_____

Country of Alps and banks:

_____

3. High, sexy heel:

_____

Really short musical note:

_____

The *T* in BLT:

_____

Snooty way to say the *T* in BLT:

_____

4. Wild animal and a sneaker:

_____

Tall blond actress who killed Bill (first name):

_____

Something heard through the grapevine:

_____

Born post '45, often an age of denial:

_____

5. What women put on their face:

_____

What you should get annually:

_____

What cars should get annually:

_____

What celebs sign before they marry:

_____

6. Egg who sat on a wall:

_____

Form of suicide, popular during WWII:

_____

African American beauty:

_____

Desperate football pass:

_____

7. Small crib:

_____

Chocolate-coated raisin:

_____

Partial, tiny kitchen:

_____

Blond Brit who played the queen and Dylan:

_____

8. Kind of singer Bing Crosby was:

_____

The Betty on cake mixes:

_____

What a saltine is:

_____

A duck is a:

_____

9. Popular online gossip site:

_____

Syndrome you may get if you grind your teeth:

_____

Place where the military and their stuff aren't supposed to be (abbrev.):

_____

What people on death row hope will prove them innocent:

_____

On the Air

★ Tongue Tipper ★

1. Who's the _____ with the _____
GOODY TWO-SHOES BLONDE   JOCK

_____ who got her start on that _____
HUSBAND   REALITY SHOW IN THE

_____ and was lucky to land a job on that _____
JUNGLE   BLABBY

_____ with the _____ who dumped the __
TALK SHOW   MOTHER HEN   ONE

_____?
WHO LOST A THOUSAND POUNDS

2. What's that _____ when
THING YOU'RE SUPPOSED TO PERFORM

someone has a heart attack that sounds like that

_____ that has that _____
RADIO NETWORK FOR LIBERALS   SHOW WITH THE

_____ who are always cracking up about engine
BROTHERS

trouble?

3. Who's that _____
FAMOUS SITCOM ACTRESS WITH THE DIABETES AND THE
_____ who got her start on the _____
SMILE   SITCOM WITH THE GUY WHO WAS A
_____ in the _____ with that
CHIMNEY SWEEP   MOVIE ABOUT THE FLYING NANNY
_____?
SONG ABOUT THE GIANT WORD

4. Who's that _____ who tells us we're all so bad and
RADIO LADY

she's so good, and she's as right-wing as that _____
KING OF THE

_____ who's even more offensive than the _____
LOUDMOUTHS   GRUMPY

_____ who made fun of that _____
RADIO GUY WITH THE HAT   WOMEN'S COLLEGE

_____ from that _____ with the _____?
BASKETBALL TEAM   STATE   GAY GOVERNOR

5. What's that _____ and the drinking,
SHOW ABOUT TWO BROTHERS

womanizing one is a _____whose
DRINKING WOMANIZER IN REAL LIFE

_____ divorced him because of it and ended up
BEAUTIFUL BLOND WIFE

for a while with the _____ of her _____
ROCKER EX-HUSBAND   BEAUTIFUL BLOND

_____ before she got her own tell-all reality show?
BEST FRIEND

6. Who's the _____ and was gay for awhile with
BLONDE WHO SAW UFOs

the _____ who married the _____
DANCING TALK SHOW BLONDE   BEAUTIFUL

_____ from the _____ with the _____
BLOND ACTRESS   TV SHOW   REALLY SKINNY

_____ and dancing baby?
LAWYER ACTRESS

7. What's that _____ that made the
CABLE STATION THAT COSTS EXTRA

series about the _____, and the _____
GROUP OF HANGERS-ON   FAMILY THAT'S

_____ and that
THE SAME RELIGION AS ROMNEY BUT WITH MORE WIVES

_____ that a lot of people think was better
BALTIMORE COP SHOW

than the _____ starring the ___, the ___, the _____, and
         MAFIA ONE   GUY   WIFE   SHRINK

the weird ending?

8. Who's the _____ who co-hosted that _____ with
            PERKY GAL   MORNING SHOW

the _____ who has the _____ and
     NEWS AND SPORTS GUY   SPORTS GUY BROTHER

then with the _____ and everybody loved
              GUY WHO'S LOSING HIS HAIR

her until she went to _____ evening ____?
                     UNCLE WHAT'S-HIS-NAME'S   SHOW

9. Who's that strangely articulate _____
                                      GUY WITH THE SLEAZY DAYTIME

_____ who's not the _____
SHOW   GUY WITH A DIFFERENT SLEAZY DAYTIME SHOW

whose name is like that ____ about how the _____ spends
                        BOOK   AUTHOR

his Tuesdays till the guy dies?

10. What's that _____, not the
                   CASINO GAME WHERE YOU SPIN THE WHEEL

_____ with _____ and that _____
TV KNOCKOFF   WHAT'S-HER-NAME   NICE GUY WHO'S

_____ almost as long as that _____ hosted that
HOSTED IT   MISS AMERICA GUY

_____, from pork rinds to
SHOW ABOUT HOW MUCH EVERYTHING COSTS

patio furniture?

11. Who's the _____ who's always sparring with the
                 AMERICAN IDOL GUY

_____?
GUY WITH THE NIPPLES

12. Who's the _____ from that _____ that
KID STAR   '70s SINGING FAMILY SHOW

was like the other _____, with a million kids and
OBNOXIOUS ONE

reunions and a movie, who keeps popping up on reality

TV shows talking about his drug problems?

13. Who's the _____ whose _____
APPLE GUY   WAY LESS FAMOUS PARTNER WITH THE

_____ hooked up for a while with that _____
FUNNY NAME   D-LIST COMEDIAN

who's as obscene as the _____ who hooked up
PRETTY JEWISH ONE

with the _____ and they all became famous?
LATE NIGHT GUY

14. Who's that _____
NEWS GUY WHOSE HAIR LOOKS OLDER THAN HE IS

whose _____ made the really tight jeans?
REALLY RICH MOTHER

15. What are those _____ that _____
SUPER-EXPENSIVE SHOES   WHAT'S-HER-NAME

wore in that _____ where they all
TV SHOW THAT BECAME A HIT MOVIE

sip that _____ that's the same name as that magazine
PINK DRINK

that young women read until they get married and start

reading the _____ or the ___
ONE WITH "CAN THIS MARRIAGE BE SAVED?"   ONE

_____?
WITH THE SEAL OF APPROVAL

★ **Take 10** ★

Cable News Guys

Who's—

1. The _____?
   ILLEGAL ALIEN FANATIC

2. The _____?
   RANTER WHO SUPPOSEDLY DOESN'T SPIN

3. The _____?
   LIBERAL WITH THE GLASSES

4. The _____?
   GUY WHOSE LAST NAME IS LIKE ONE OF SANTA'S REINDEER

5. The _____?
   HOT MONEY CHICK

6. The _____ with the _____ that sounds like it should
   UPBEAT PUNDIT   SHOW
   be on ESPN but it's not?

7. The _____?
   HYPER MONEY GUY

8. The _____?
   HYPER IDEA GUY

9. The _____?
   BLONDE WHO DISPPEARED AFTER HER MARRIAGE SCANDAL

10. The _____?
    SPORTS GUYS WITH THE SAME FIRST NAME

★ Take 10 ★

Celebrity Chefs

Who's—

1. The _____?
   SUPER-TALL AMERICAN FRENCH CHEF WITH THE WARBLY VOICE

2. The _____?
   FARM LADY WITH THE MEASURING CUP

3. The _____?
   OVER-BUBBLY, OVEREXPOSED TV CHEF

4. The _____?
   CHUBBY, CHUCKLING SOUTHERN WOMAN WITH THE SONS

5. The _____?
   CUTE NAKED BRIT

6. The _____?
   "BAM" GUY

7. The _____ with the _____
   LOVELY ITALIAN AMERICAN   FAMOUS MOVIE PRODUCER
   _____?
   GRANDFATHER

8. The _____ of the _____?
   INDIAN EX-WIFE   SATANIC VERSES GUY

9. The ____ who started that _____
   GUY   RESTAURANT CHAIN WHERE THEY
   _____?
   ALWAYS THROW SHRIMP AROUND

10. The _____?
    CHEF IN THE CAN

Art History 101

★ Tongue Tipper ★

1. Who's that _____ whose name

OVERRATED SPORTS ARTIST

sounds like that _____ and you always see

STAR TREK ACTOR

his prints in the urologist's office?

2. Who's the _____

ARTIST WITH THE SPLATTER PAINTINGS

_____ whose first

EVERYONE SAYS THEIR 5-YEAR-OLD COULD DO

name is like that _____ and a

FAMOUS HAMBURGER JOINT

city in that _____ out west with the

RECTANGULAR STATE

____ that has that _____?

PARK   WATER SPURTING OUT OF IT

3. What's that _____ whose commercials still

CARD COMPANY

show Dad in that _____ that jolts back

FAKE LEATHER CHAIR

while he's holding that _____ and he
SHERLOCK HOLMES-Y THING

looks straight out of an illustration by the _____
SATURDAY EVENING

_____?
POST GUY

4. Who's the _____ with that _____ by
ARTIST WITH THE EAR   SONG ABOUT HIM

the ___ who wrote that other _____
GUY   SONG ABOUT THE "CHEVY TO

_____ that has the same title as that funny but gross
THE LEVEE"

movie with that _____ and the sequels?
BLOND PARTY-GIRL ACTRESS

5. Who's the _____
JEWISH ARTIST WHO PAINTED THE PEOPLE FLOATING IN THE

___ like that _____ that people see if they can't get
AIR   CIRCUS IN VEGAS

tickets to see the _____?
CANADIAN SINGER WHO FINALLY HAD A BABY

6. What are those two icicle things in caves and _____
ONE HANGS

_____ and the other's _____ and families take
FROM THE TOP   ON THE BOTTOM

long car trips to see them in that _____ in the ____
CAVERN PLACE   STATE

where the _____ and
WOMAN PAINTED BONES AND GIGANTIC FLOWERS

was as famous as the _____ who painted
WOMAN WITH THE UNIBROW

_____?
MUCH FARTHER SOUTH

7. Who's the ____ who did that _____
ARTIST   NAKED SCULPTURE OF THE

_____ who was facing the ____ whose name
SLINGSHOT GUY   GIANT

sounds like you're saying it with a speech impediment?

8. What's that _____
GLOPPY SANDWICH WITH CORNED BEEF AND RUSSIAN
_____ that sounds like the _____ who painted women
DRESSING   ARTIST
who look like they'd been eating a lot of those sandwiches

and maybe some ice cream sundaes, too?

9. Who's the _____
ARTIST WITH THE DOTS AND THE COMIC BOOK PEOPLE
whose name is like that _____ that you
TINY COUNTRY IN EUROPE
could easily confuse with that _____
OTHER TINY COUNTRY IN EUROPE
that starts with the same letter and sounds a little like that

_____?
OLD BRAND OF SOAP

10. Who's the _____ who painted in the factory
SOUP CAN GUY
but spent more time in that _____ before he died in
PLACE
that _____ he was scared to death of?
OTHER KIND OF PLACE

★ SOUND ALIKES V ★

Fill in the blanks with words that sound alike, more or less. Sometimes less.

1. Fuel that trucks use:

_____

What you also do when you razzle:

_____

Kind of woman in distress:

_____

African American superstar (first name):

_____

2. Game you play on a big plastic mat with colorful circles on it:

_____

Sibling who is a female:

_____

Wine with soda in it:

_____

Last name of Client 9:

_____

3. Language in Mexico:

_____

Popeye's vegetable:

_____

Congressman Newt's last name:

_____

Book of World Records:

_____

4. 1960s housewife tranquilizer:

_____

Place the Pope lives:

_____

Healthy pill you take daily:

_____

Least popular war before Iraq:

_____

5. The Beatles' "Eleanor":

_____

Sport more primitive than football:

_____

Mr. Believe It or Not:

_____

Gum maker and famous baseball field:

_____

6. Game that upper-crust English people play with mallets and balls and then they drink tea:

_____

Little breaded salmon patties (or chicken balls, for that matter):

_____

Really short, military-type haircut:

_____

Salami, baloney, etc.:

_____

7. Childhood disease caused by lack of sunlight:

_____

Framed equipment used by tennis and squash players:

_____

Women who kick their legs in unison, especially around Christmas:

_____

Things in the anthem with the red glare:

_____

8. Birthday decorations that are tied to chairs or hang from the ceiling:

_____

Large monkeys:

_____

Woodwind instruments that look sort of like big clarinets:

_____

Funny name for breasts:

_____

9. Form of Japanese comic book:

_____

Italian word for eat:

_____

Tropical fruit:

_____

Latin dance:

_____

All Over the Map

★ Tongue Tipper ★

1. What's the ____ with the _____ with the heads?
STATE · MOUNTAIN

2. What's the ___ where that _____ left his heart and
CITY · SINGER

probably some of that _____?
RICE MIX

3. What's that _____ where every year some
SPANISH TOWN

American gets trampled that the _____
MACHO GUY WITH THE

_____ loved almost as much as that _____
SHORT SENTENCES · SNOWY

_____ and going after that _____
MOUNTAIN IN AFRICA · BIG, FAT FISH

that sounds like the _____?
BIG, FAT *GODFATHER* GUY

4. What's that _____?
GREAT LAKE WITH THE SPOOKY NAME

5. What's that ____ with the white cliffs and the ___ that's
          PLACE   FISH

good with lemon that's near that _____ people swim across
                          WATER

and drown in, and it's in the same country as that ___
                                     OLD

_____ that has nothing to do with that _____
GROUP OF ROCKS   REALLY OLD

_____ with the _____?
ROCK GROUP   GUY WITH THE LIPS

6. What's that old _____ where everyone went to
                HONEYMOON PLACE

commit suicide and that _____ sounds just like it?
                      BLUE PILL

7. What's that _____ and the _____
          BIG TEXAS CITY WITH THE ASTROS   STADIUM

where that _____ totally tanked and everyone got screwed
          COMPANY

and didn't even get to see the _____
                        CEO WHOSE LAST NAME SOUNDS

_____ go to jail because he died?
LIKE A POTATO CHIP

8. What's that _____ that's right above the
          COUNTRY WITH THE CLOGS

_____ and the ___ named for those
COUNTRY WITH THE CHOCOLATE   CITY

_____and where the people
VEGETABLES THAT LOOK LIKE MINI CABBAGES

speak that _____ that sounds like the _____
          LANGUAGE   STUFF GUNKING UP

_____ when you have a cold?
YOUR THROAT

9. Who's the _____ who's buried in the
          DEAD GUY FROM THE DOORS

same cemetery in that ___ as the _____, and
                  CITY   "LA VIE EN ROSE" LADY

Americans visit him, unlike the _____, who
                                DEAD GRATEFUL DEAD GUY

everybody eats as an _____, thanks to those _____
_{ICE CREAM FLAVOR}   _{OTHER}

_____?
_{TWO GUYS}

10. What's that _____ that used to be Burma but now its
_{COUNTRY}

name sounds like one of those _____?
_{SHINY BALLOONS}

11. What's that ____ on that _____flag that comes from
_{LEAF}   _{COLD COUNTRY'S}

the tree with the _____ you pour on those _____
_{STICKY STUFF}   _{PANCAKE-LIKE}

_____?
_{LIKE THINGS WITH SQUARE INDENTATIONS}

12. What's that _____—
_{OLD-FASHIONED RELIGIOUS SECT IN PENNSYLVANIA}

not the _____—that looks just like the ____
_{OATMEAL PEOPLE}   _{OLD-}

_____, except the Pennsylvanians
_{FASHIONED JEWISH SECT IN BROOKLYN}

ride _____ to get around and the Jews take the
_{HORSE THINGS}

subway?

13. What's the _____ that's in the same
_{PLACE THAT ALL ROADS LEAD TO}

_____ as the _____ that has all of those ____
_{COUNTRY}   _{CITY WITHOUT ROADS}   _{BOATS}

and tourists and sounds like _____?
_{DEER MEAT}

14. What's that _____ that's the name of a city in that
_{KIND OF ENVELOPE}

_____ where the _____ was the dictator?
_{COUNTRY}   _{LADY WITH THE SHOES}

15. What's the _____ that's also a _____
                   COUNTRY IN SOUTH AMERICA   GREAT SPICY

_____, but not the _____
SUPER BOWL PARTY FOOD WITH BEANS   LIGHT-COLORED

____ that's spelled like the capital of that other _____
BEAN   COUNTRY

_____?
DOWN THERE

16. What's that _____ in that _____
                   CITY WITH THE FAMOUS WALTZ   COUNTRY WHERE

_____ that isn't the _____ with
THE HILLS ARE ALIVE   MOUNTAINOUS COUNTRY

the _____ and the _____ and the _____
     KNIVES   CHEESE   GIRL WITH THE BRAIDS

where they do that weird throat singing that's become an

_____?
AFTER-SCHOOL SNACK

17. What's that _____ where the _____ helped the
                   PLACE IN INDIA   SAINT LADY

people with that _____ that sort of sounds like those ____
                 DISEASE   LITTLE

_____ who eat Lucky Charms?
GREEN IRISH PEOPLE

★ **Take 10** ★

Greats

What's—

1. The _____?
NAME OF THE GREEK CONQUEROR

2. That _____?
OLD CHINESE TOURIST ATTRACTION

3. That _____?
BIG AMUSEMENT PARK

4. The _____?
STEVE MCQUEEN MOVIE WITH THE MOTORCYCLE CHASE

5. That _____?
BIG BREED OF DOG LIKE MARMADUKE

6. That _____
ERA WHEN THERE WERE ALL THOSE BREAD LINES AND NOBODY
_____?
COULD SPARE A DIME

7. That _____
SONG THAT MADE THE GUY WHO MARRIED HIS 13-YEAR-OLD
_____?
COUSIN FAMOUS

8. The _____
BRAGGING NAME FOR RINGLING BROS. AND BARNUM &
_____?
BAILEY CIRCUS

9. What _____?
ALI CALLS HIMSELF

10. The _____?
FAMOUS GET-OUT-OF-HANDCUFFS MAGICIAN

★ **Take 10** ★

Magnificent Sevens

What's—

1. That _____?
   GROUP OF SNOW WHITE'S BUDDIES

2. That _____?
   GANG OF GREED, SLOTH, AND ALL THOSE OTHER GUYS

3. The _____
   MUSICAL WHERE ALL THOSE RELATIVES GET MARRIED IN
   _____?
   TECHNICOLOR

4. That _____?
   SITCOM WITH THE MINISTER AND JESSICA BIEL

5. The _____?
   ITCH THAT MARRIED PEOPLE GET

6. The _____?
   RELIGIOUS DENOMINATION THAT RINGS YOUR DOORBELL

7. The _____?
   CLASSIC KUROSAWA FILM WITH SWORDS

8. That _____?
   BOOK ABOUT ALL THOSE HABITS WE SHOULD HAVE

9. That _____?
   GROUP OF WORDS THAT THE COMEDIAN GOT IN TROUBLE FOR

10. That _____?
    LATE-IN-THE-GAME STADIUM EXERCISE

Kids' Stuff

★ Tongue Tipper ★

1. What's that _____ that's also the
STUFF IN A THERMOMETER
name of a little planet, but not as little as the _____
PLANET
_____ with the same name as the Disney
THAT GOT DEMOTED
dog that's not the _____ and they both
CLUMSY DISNEY DOG
hang out with the _____ and that _____?
MOUSE   ANNOYING DUCK

2. What's that _____
PRESCHOOL MUSICAL INSTRUMENT KIDS CRASH
_____ and the other _____ that the
TOGETHER   ONE WITH THE SHAPE
least musical kid gets to tap once or twice when they're

performing the song about the ____ or the ____?
STAR   SHEEP

3. Who's that _____ in that nurs-
GUY WHO COULD EAT NO FAT
ery rhyme written either by that _____ or those
OLD LADY

_____ whose characters always end up almost
UNHAPPY BROTHERS

being eaten by wolves or witches, like the _____
                                            GIRL WITH THE

_____ and the _____ with the crumbs?
GRANDMOTHER   BROTHER AND SISTER

4. Who's that _____ all moms want to smash, unlike
                  PURPLE DINOSAUR

those _____ who live together on the _____
      TWO GUY MUPPETS   TV STATION

that brought us that other _____?
                            PURPLE CHARACTER WITH THE PURSE

5. Who's that _____ at _____
                  CUB REPORTER/PHOTOGRAPHER   SUPERMAN'S

_____ whose name sounds like that _____
NEWSPAPER   MORALIZING

_____ in the movie about the _____?
CRICKET   WOODEN KID WITH THE NOSE

6. What are those _____ that sound like those
                      FAT GERMAN SAUSAGES

_____ that are the
DOLLS THAT LOOK LIKE SLUTTY VERSIONS OF BARBIE

exact opposite of those _____
                        GOODY-GOODY EXPENSIVE DOLLS WITH THE

_____ and the ___ that stars the _____?
BOOKS   FILM   LITTLE MISS SUNSHINE GIRL

7. What's that _____
                  TYPE OF BIG DINOSAUR WITH THE LONG NECK AND TAIL

that _____ in the _____ used to ride
     WHAT'S-HIS-NAME   PREHISTORIC CARTOON

on at his construction job and then they made his _____
                                                  DAUGHTER

into a disgustingly sweet breakfast cereal?

8. Who's that _____ who was a
                  FAMOUS POTATO WITH THE MUSTACHE AND HAT

sidekick in that _____ with the _____ whose
                 FIRST PIXAR FLICK   ASTRONAUT TOY

voice was done by the _____ who has made a
HOME IMPROVEMENT GUY
million Christmas movies?

9. Who's that _____ who
STEAL-FROM-THE-RICH/GIVE-TO-THE-POOR GUY
lived in the woods and dressed like that _____ who never
BOY MAN
grows up and lives with that _____ who has the same name
FAIRY
as that _____ tiny dog?
RICH BLONDE'S

10. What is that _____ that comes in a
STUFF THAT LOOKS LIKE MUCUS
jar with a stick that they still sell at office-supply stores,

right near that _____ you make circles with and the
POINTY THING
_____ you use to measure angles in the _____
HALF CIRCLE CLASS THAT ISN'T
_____?
ALGEBRA

11. What's that _____ in every pediatrician's office that
KIDS' MAGAZINE
you read before you graduate to the _____ with
FUNNY MAGAZINE
that _____ on the cover who looks like George W.
FRECKLED GUY
Bush mixed with that _____ and
LATE NIGHT, GAP-TOOTHED COMEDIAN
also with the _____ who's got the ___
LATE LATE ONE WITH THE RED HAIR ONE
_____ job next?
WITH THE CHIN'S

★ SOUND ALIKES VI ★

Fill in the blanks with words that sound alike, more or less.
Sometimes less.

1. Second fiddle to Google:

_____

That slightly fizzy chocolate milk drink:

_____

Doll you stick pins in:

_____

What you put a cute Band-Aid on:

_____

2. Thing all Texans are supposed to remember:

_____

What you have to pay when you divorce:

_____

What you have to pay when you divorce but were never
really married:

_____

Golden horse:

_____

3. Island that immigrants came through:

_____

Girl who went through the looking glass:

_____

Big book of maps:

_____

What someone without a hat is:

_____

4. Sound of a doorbell:

_____

Game with little balls that get dented:

_____

Whiny voice kids sometimes talk in:

_____

Movie that never looks realistic, no matter how many times they remake it:

_____

5. Ravi Shankar's singing daughter's last name:

_____

Girl burned at the stake's first name:

_____

Boy band brothers:

_____

Bible guy with the whale:

_____

6. Parthenon country:

_____

Oversize ducks:

_____

Person who calls someone young a "whippersnapper":

_____

Place where the steam comes out of the earth:

_____

7. Popular, round, orange-colored cracker:

_____

Unpopular rodents:

_____

People from Britain:

_____

Spoiled kids:

_____

8. Last name of the guy who wrote the _Portnoy_ book:

_____

Babe's last name:

_____

Round thing you hang on the door at Christmas:

_____

The Grapes of:

_____

9. Game you play in church basements:

_____

Kind of African drum:

_____

Dumb blonde:

_____

Game where you bend under the broom:

_____

Science Fair

★ Tongue Tipper ★

1. What's that _____ with the spores that
DEADLY WHITE STUFF

sounds like the name of the _____?
NATIONAL TRAIN SYSTEM

2. Who's the famous _____ who discovered gravity
SCIENTIST

when he saw that _____ fall and his
FRUIT THAT'S A COMPUTER

last name is the last name of a _____?
COOKIE

3. Who's the _____ in the movie
GIRL WITH ALL THOSE PERSONALITIES

who had almost the same disease as the mathematician

in that _____ with the _____ and both
OTHER MOVIE   GLADIATOR ACTOR

conditions get lumped together with that _____ that
DISORDER

sounds like those _____?
WHITE BEARS WHO ARE ALL DROWNING

4. What was that _____
FIRST SPACE MISSION THAT WENT TO THE MOON

with the _____ who said something about _____
ASTRONAUT   STEPPING ON

_____ that shares the same name with that other _____
MANKIND   MISSION

_____ where it looked like the three guys
WITH ANOTHER NUMBER

were going to die but they didn't so they made a movie

about it with the _____ and _____ guys?
FORREST GUMP   SIX DEGREES

5. What are those _____ the fortune tellers use when they're
CARDS

not using that ____ to tell you that you're going to go on a
BALL

long journey because that _____
CONSTELLATION WITH THE GUY WITH THE

_____ is in the house of the _____ with
JUG OF WATER   PLANET WITH THE RINGS

that _____ rising?
SIGN WITH THE FISH

6. Who's that _____ who has the same
KID IN PEANUTS WITH THE BLANKET

first name as the _____
GUY WHO DISCOVERED THAT VITAMIN C IS GOOD

_____, just like that _____ that sounds like what
FOR A COLD   OTHER PLANT

it's called _____
WHEN YOU PULL THE PLUG ON SOMEONE WHO'S GOING TO

_____ (but not from a cold)?
DIE ANYWAY

7. What's the ____ that gives you good luck and the other
LEAF

_____ that give you bad rashes and then you have to
THREE LEAVES

put on the _____ that sounds like the _____
PINK LOTION   HIGH SCHOOL WITH

_____?
THE MASSACRE

8. What's that _____
TROPICAL DISEASE THAT SOUNDS LIKE A CUTE JUICE

_____ that's carried by that _____?
FLAVOR   FLY WITH THE FUNNY NAME

9. What's that _____ that sounds like the _____
TYPE OF ROCK   COCKROACH NOVEL

by the _____ almost everybody reads in high
EXISTENTIAL ANGST GUY

school after they read the _____ by the _____?
TEEN ANGST ONE   RECLUSE

10. What's that _____ that sounds like the
INSECT WITH ALL THE LEGS

_____ of the _____?
INCH-LIKE PART   MEASUREMENT SYSTEM WE DON'T USE

11. Who are _____ until
THOSE PEOPLE WHO ALWAYS THINK THEY'RE SICK

someone gives them that _____ that sounds like _____
FAKE PILL   ONE OF

_____?
THOSE THREE ITALIAN TENORS

★ Take 10 ★

Is There a Doctor in the House?

Who—

1. _____?
   PUT THE CAT IN THE HAT

2. _____?
   MAKES ALL OF THE SHOE INSERTS

3. _____?
   WROTE THE BABY BOOK

4. _____?
   TRADED OFF WITH MR. HYDE

5. _____?
   WASN'T DR. YES

6. _____?
   TALKED TO ANIMALS

7. _____?
   WAS THE FIRST ONE TO LEAVE OPRAH'S PRACTICE TO START HIS OWN

8. ____?
   RAPS

9. _____?
   IS SHERLOCK'S SIDEKICK

10. _____?
    COMES IN A BOTTLE OR CAN

★ Take 10 ★

Greek Myths and Legends

Who's—

1. The _____?
   BABY WITH THE ARROW

2. The _____?
   GUY WITH THE LIGHTNING BOLT

3. The _____?
   STRONG ONE

4. The _____?
   GUY WITH THE GLOBE

5. The _____?
   LADY WITH THE BOX

6. The _____?
   GUY WITH THE HEEL

7. The _____?
   MUSIC GUY WITH THE THEATER IN HARLEM THAT'S ON TV

8. The _____?
   GUY WHO IS AN EXPENSIVE SCARF AND HANDBAG

9. The _____?
   GUY WHO BECAME A CRUISE SHIP AND A DISASTER MOVIE

10. The _____?
    GUY WITH AN EYE IN THE MIDDLE

Good Eats

★ Tongue Tipper ★

1. What's that _____ that tastes

GALAXY THAT'S ALSO A CANDY BAR

just like the other _____ that

CANDY BAR WITH THE THREE GUYS

sounds like the _____?

TV KIDS WITH THE EARS

2. What's that _____, when

LONG, SKINNY BREAD THEY EAT IN PARIS

they're not downing those _____

BUTTERY HALF-MOON PASTRIES

with all the calories, and they wear those _____

FLAT LITTLE

____, just like that famous _____?

HATS   FRENCH GUY WHO DIDN'T TALK

3. Who's the _____ who overused the _____ from

     DIET LADY   ACTRESS

the _____ and then the _____

SHOW WITH THE BAR AND THE SONG   OTHER

_____ whose last name sounds like the _____ who

ACTRESS   OLIVE OIL

was married to the _____, and then she overused the _____
               ROCKER   RAPPER/

_____?
ACTRESS/ROLE MODEL

4. What's that _____ that you could break a
            REALLY GRAVEL-LIKE CEREAL

molar on that's eaten by the same folks who buy the _____
                                            HIPPIE

_____ or that other _____
CEREAL   CEREAL THAT LOOKS LIKE SCRATCHY BROWN

_____?
PILLOWS

5. What's that ____ you kill in November that's also a country
            BIRD

that used to be head of that _____ that's also a
                        BIG ANCIENT EMPIRE

footrest, and it's right next to the _____
                               COUNTRY THAT SOUNDS LIKE

_____?
WHAT'S LEFT ON YOUR HANDS AFTER YOU'VE EATEN FRIES

6. What's that _____
           CHOCOLATE-COATED ICE CREAM BAR WITHOUT A STICK

named for the _____ who live in those _____
              PEOPLE   DOMES MADE OF SNOW

who eat that _____ and have sled dogs like that _____
              WHALE STUFF   FAMOUS

_____?
ONE WITH THE SERUM AND THE MOVIE

7. Who's that _____
           LADY WHO MAKES OVERPRICED CHOCOLATE CHIP COOKIES

who probably hates the _____
                  LADY WHO MAKES PRETZELS AT THE MALL

and they probably both hate the one _____?
                             NOBODY DOESN'T LIKE

8. What's that _____ that got everyone
            BUBBLY FRENCH WATER

thinking water should be fancy, so then they started

drinking the _____, and the
<u>ITALIAN WATER IN THE GREEN BOTTLES</u>

water from that _____
<u>SPRING THAT SOUNDS LIKE IT'S IN EASTERN</u>

_____ and the _____ from
<u>EUROPE BUT IT'S NOT</u>   <u>WATER IN THE SQUARE BOTTLE</u>

that island where there used to be cannibals?

9. What's that _____ that's popular because,
<u>FRUIT WITH THE RED SEEDS</u>

if you drink the juice, you're supposed to live as long as

that _____, unlike the _____ famous
<u>REALLY OLD BIBLE GUY</u>   <u>OTHER BIBLE GUY</u>

for dying young because his _____ killed him?
<u>BROTHER</u>

10. Who's the _____ who sounds like the _____
<u>OLD VEGAS PERFORMER</u>   <u>BREAD</u>

you buy at a deli?

11. What's that 1970s _____
<u>WEDDING GIFT WITH THE STICKS AND THE</u>

_____ that would always burn you and the _____
<u>CHEESE</u>   <u>STUFF IN THE</u>

_____ you heated it with sounds like that _____
<u>LITTLE CAN</u>   <u>SHOCK JOCK</u>

_____?
<u>WITH THE LONG HAIR AND THE STRIPPER OBSESSION</u>

12. What's that _____ that's
<u>PASTA THAT LOOKS LIKE FLATTENED SPAGHETTI</u>

always served with that _____ that sounds
<u>REALLY RICH CREAM SAUCE</u>

like a _____?
<u>FANCY ITALIAN CAR</u>

13. What's that _____ that looks like a little
<u>REALLY ROUGH CRACKER</u>

woven welcome mat?

★ SOUND ALIKES VII ★

Fill in the blanks with words that sound alike, more or less. Sometimes less.

1. Kind of light you see on liquor store and diner signs:

_____

Stuff that keeps your refrigerator cold:

_____

Lowly serf and/or office worker:

_____

Ponce de:

_____

2. Aviator with kidnapped kid:

_____

Blimp that blew up:

_____

Stinky German cheese:

_____

Mainstay of American diet:

_____

3. Wrinkly little *Star Wars* guy:

_____

Class where you try to become a lotus:

_____

Mr. Berra:

_____

Big, fat submarine sandwich:

_____

4. Thing Indians lived in that's not a wigwam:

_____

Fake hair for men:

_____

Murdered poet/rapper:

_____

Skinny stick you poke your teeth with:

_____

5. Safe Swedish car:

_____

Lord of the Rings character:

_____

Extinct bird:

_____

Stick you jump up and down on:

_____

6. Substance that can kill Superman:

_____

Very tough brand of luggage:

_____

Stuff that goes boom:

_____

Gross Australian food:

_____

7. Headache pill that's also good for your heart:

_____

Place where you ski if you're rich:

_____

Robbins' 31-flavor ice cream partner:

_____

Thing you eat with eggs that you shouldn't:

_____

8. Sport with lassos and maybe a gay cowboy:

_____

Thing everyone used to sit in front of before TV:

_____

Sandwich cookie with the best part in the middle:

_____

What you add to your pizza in restaurants because it's right there on the table:

_____

9. Last name of _In Cold Blood_ writer:

_____

The Wile E. guy in cartoons:

_____

Magic mushroom Indians and hippies used:

_____

The Prime of Miss:

_____

Gifts, Games, Gadgets, and Stuff

★ Tongue Tipper ★

1. What's that _____ that's so much
WATCH THAT KEEPS ON TICKING

cheaper than the _____ that sounds like
SUPER-FANCY WATCH

those _____ you take for an upset stomach?
CHEWABLE PILLS

2. What's that _____ that's the
SEX-DRENCHED GUY DEODORANT

adolescent equivalent of the _____ with the
AFTERSHAVE

clipper ship on the bottle that grizzled old men

splash on their faces?

3. What's that _____
GAME WITH THE LIGHTS AND THE NOISE AND

_____ you can still find in dives where they have
THE "TILT"

that _____ with the music that you put your
OTHER THING

money in that's always playing songs by the ___
GUY

_____ or else by the
WITH THE GRAY BRAID WHO DIDN'T PAY HIS TAXES

_____ with that _____
NEW JERSEY GUY   BAND NAMED AFTER A LETTER OF THE

_____?
ALPHABET

4. What's the _____ and always gets you
THING THAT WATERS LAWNS

soaked that looks like the _____ that the
MUSICAL INSTRUMENT

_____ who was kidnapped plays?
MORMON GIRL

5. What's that _____ everyone thinks
FILL-IN-THE-NUMBERS PUZZLE

everyone else is pronouncing wrong that's as popular as

the _____ that everyone thinks makes them
FILL-IN-THE-WORD PUZZLE

smart?

6. What's that _____ that everybody
CLACKING PRE-COMPUTER MACHINE

wrote on that's disappeared along with the _____
PAPER THAT GOT

_____ and that _____ that was supposed
YOUR FINGERS FILTHY   GLUMPY STUFF

to erase your mistakes but made them look worse?

7. What's that ____ that goes on forever with the houses and
GAME

hotels and everyone wants to get those _____
TWO EXPENSIVE BLUE

_____, and you always feel like a loser if you get the
PROPERTIES

_____?
RAILROAD THAT SOUNDS LIKE BODY ODOR

8. What's that _____ that's also a science
GAME KIDS PLAY WITH A STRING

fiction novel by the _____ who was as
SLAUGHTERHOUSE-FIVE GUY

freaked out by war as the _____ with the _____
AUTHOR   BESTSELLING TITLE

_____?
WITH THAT NO-WIN PHRASE

9. What's that _____ with the pimps and the drug deal-
VIDEO GAME

ers that famous actors do voice-overs for, just like they do

for that _____ with the _____ whose
CARTOON   DAD WITH THE DOUGHNUTS

name is the same as that ancient blind guy with that _____
LONG

_____ and its _____?
GREEK POEM   SEQUEL

10. What's that _____ with the tiles played by all the
CHINESE GAME

women in Florida, who make fruit salad or molds of that

_____?
JIGGLY STUFF YOU GET IN HOSPITALS

★ Take 10 ★

Name That Game Show

What's—

1. The _____?
ONE WITH THE ANSWERS

2. The _____?
ONE WITH THE ARGUING CLANS

3. The _____?
ONE WITH THE SMART KIDS AND STUPID GROWN-UPS

4. The _____?
ONE WITH THE LIE DETECTOR AND THE TRASHY QUESTIONS

5. The _____?
ONE WITH THE LIFE LINES

6. The _____?
ONE WITH THE BRIEFCASES

7. The _____?
OLD ONE WITH THE ISOLATION BOOTH AND THE SCANDAL

8. The _____?
ONE WITH THE BACHELORS OR BACHELORETTES ON STOOLS

9. The _____
ONE WHERE COUPLES REALIZE THEY DON'T KNOW EACH
_____?
OTHER VERY WELL

10. The _____?
ONE WITH CELEBRITIES IN BOXES

★ Take 10 ★

Games People Play

What's—

1. The _____?
   ONE WITH THE BALL ATTACHED TO THE POLE

2. The _____?
   ONE PEOPLE PLAY ON BEACHES TO SHOW OFF THEIR PERFECT BODIES

3. The _____?
   ONE WHERE YOU THROW THE PLASTIC PLATE, SOMETIMES TO A DOG

4. The _____?
   ONE WHERE YOU HOP AROUND THE SQUARES

5. The _____
   ONE WHERE YOU'RE IN THE MIDDLE AND CAN'T GET THE BALL AND
   _____?
   IT STARTS TO FEEL PERSONAL

6. The _____?
   ONE WHERE KIDS CHEAT BY SQUINTING THROUGH THEIR FINGERS

7. The _____?
   ONE WHERE KIDS CHEAT BY PEEKING UNDER THE BLINDFOLD

8. The _____?
   ONE WHERE YOU HIT YOUR FRIENDS WITH BALLS

9. The _____?
   ONE WHERE YOU GIVE YOUR FRIENDS CONCUSSIONS

10. The _____?
    ONE WHERE YOU YELL THE ITALIAN GUY'S NAME IN THE POOL

Lightning Round

★ The One That's Not ★

Sometimes when you're looking for a word, a name, or a place, you can only come up with the thing it's not—something close, but wrong. "Who's the one that's not Al Pacino?" It's Robert DeNiro!

Okay, you get it. Think of this as a lightning round. See how fast you can go.

Round I

What's—

1. The _____?
ONE THAT'S NOT BULIMIA

2. The _____?
ONE THAT'S NOT A HAMSTER

3. The _____?
ONE THAT'S NOT JON STEWART

4. The _____?
ONE THAT'S NOT A FIG

5. The _____?
ONE THAT'S NOT AN OYSTER

6. The _____?
ONE THAT'S NOT FOX NEWS

7. The _____?
ONE THAT'S NOT THE MOONIES

8. The _____?
ONE THAT'S NOT POKÉMON

9. The _____?
ONE THAT'S NOT PAUL NEWMAN

10. The _____?
ONE THAT'S NOT SERENA

11. The _____?
ONE THAT'S NOT MARBLE

12. The _____?
ONE THAT'S NOT MANSLAUGHTER

13. The _____?
ONE THAT'S NOT ASTRONOMY

14. The _____?
ONE THAT'S NOT CREDIT

15. The _____?
ONE THAT'S NOT MEASLES

16. The _____?
ONE THAT'S NOT BOSWELL

17. The _____?
ONE THAT'S NOT THELMA

18. The _____?
ONE THAT'S NOT ANALOG

19. The _____?
ONE THAT'S NOT SALAMI

20. The _____?
ONE THAT'S NOT DEAN MARTIN

Round II

What's—

1. The _____?
   ONE THAT'S NOT DELILAH

2. The _____?
   ONE THAT'S NOT SARDINES?

3. The _____?
   ONE THAT'S NOT MICHELANGELO

4. The _____?
   ONE THAT'S NOT GREENLAND

5. The _____?
   ONE THAT'S NOT LIVINGSTON

6. The _____?
   ONE THAT'S NOT YALE

7. The _____?
   ONE THAT'S NOT CHECKERS

8. The _____?
   ONE THAT'S NOT A TROMBONE

9. The _____?
   ONE THAT'S NOT LATIN

10. The _____?
    ONE THAT'S NOT HAWAII

11. The _____?
    ONE THAT'S NOT THE DISCOVERY CHANNEL

12. The _____?
    ONE THAT'S NOT AFT

13. The _____?
    ONE THAT'S NOT A SCYTHE

14. The _____?
    ONE THAT'S NOT HETEROGENEOUS

15. The _____?
    ONE THAT'S NOT A SPEEDOMETER

16. The _____?
ONE THAT'S NOT YANG

17. The _____?
ONE THAT'S NOT ACETAMINOPHEN

18. The _____?
ONE THAT'S NOT GALILEO

19. The _____?
ONE THAT'S NOT NESTLÉ

20. The _____?
ONE THAT'S NOT THE ARCTIC

Round III

What's—

1. The _____?
ONE THAT'S NOT DANIEL BOONE

2. The _____?
ONE THAT'S NOT THE CUBAN MISSILE CRISIS

3. The _____?
ONE THAT'S NOT ABU DHABI

4. The _____?
ONE THAT'S NOT FEDEX

5. The _____?
ONE THAT'S NOT *NEWSWEEK*

6. The _____?
ONE THAT'S NOT A VIOLIN

7. The _____?
ONE THAT'S NOT MALIA

8. The _____?
ONE THAT'S NOT *I DREAM OF JEANNIE*

9. The _____?
ONE THAT'S NOT A PIE

10. The _____?
ONE THAT'S NOT THE SUWANNEE RIVER

11. The _____?
ONE THAT'S NOT WAFFLES

12. The _____?
ONE THAT'S NOT THE CIA

13. The _____?
ONE THAT'S NOT CHICHEN ITZA

14. The _____?
ONE THAT'S NOT AJAX

15. The _____?
ONE THAT'S NOT YUGOSLAVIA

16. The _____?
ONE THAT'S NOT JESSE HELMS

17. The _____?
ONE THAT'S NOT SYPHILIS

18. The _____?
ONE THAT'S NOT SEATTLE

19. The _____?
ONE THAT'S NOT MANET

20. The _____?
ONE THAT'S NOT CHITA RIVERA

Round IV

What's—

1. The _____?
ONE THAT'S NOT *PLAYBOY*

2. The _____?
ONE THAT'S NOT FAHRENHEIT

3. The _____?
   ONE THAT'S NOT THE LAMBADA

4. The _____?
   ONE THAT'S NOT JIF

5. The _____?
   ONE THAT'S NOT HONEYDEW

6. The _____?
   ONE THAT'S NOT BEER

7. The _____?
   ONE THAT'S NOT A CROCODILE

8. The _____?
   ONE THAT'S NOT A WEREWOLF

9. The _____?
   ONE THAT'S NOT RIN TIN TIN

10. The _____?
    ONE THAT'S NOT MRS. BUTTERWORTH

11. The _____?
    ONE THAT'S NOT BACTERIAL

12. The _____?
    ONE THAT'S NOT SALON.COM

13. The _____?
    ONE THAT'S NOT FLORA

14. The _____?
    ONE THAT'S NOT SUSHI

15. The _____?
    ONE THAT'S NOT AN OTTER

16. The _____?
    ONE THAT'S NOT DOSTOYEVSKY

17. The _____?
    ONE THAT'S NOT FRANKENSTEIN

18. The _____?
ONE THAT'S NOT THE TROPIC OF CANCER

19. The _____?
ONE THAT'S NOT FREDDIE MAC

20. The _____?
ONE THAT'S NOT FERNANDO LAMAS

The uh . . . thing when a book is over. When the pages stop. The thing that's not the beginning. Or the middle, even. The . . .

END! That's it.

The end.

Answer Key

SCORING: Each blank counts for ONE POINT. Add FIVE BONUS POINTS for every Tongue Tipper or Sound Alike where you correctly filled in all the blanks. Add FIVE BONUS POINTS for correctly filling in all questions in a Take 10 round. Add FIVE BONUS POINTS if you correctly filled in all questions in a lightning round of the One That's Not.

Tongue Tipper: Reel Life

1. Meg Ryan, *Sleepless in Seattle*, *When Harry Met Sally*, Russell Crowe, Dennis Quaid, Randy Quaid
2. Charlton Heston, *Ben Hur*, Bengay
3. Reese's Pieces, *E.T.*, Reese Witherspoon, June Carter Cash, Johnny Cash
4. *Terms of Endearment*, Jack Nicholson, Shirley Maclaine, Debra Winger
5. *Deliverance*, "Dueling Banjos"
6. Francis Ford Coppola, Sophia Coppola, *Lost in Translation*, Bill Murray, Scarlett Johansson
7. *Dirty Dancing*, Patrick Swayze, Jennifer Grey, Jerry Orbach, Joel Grey
8. Susan Sarandon, Tim Robbins, *Bull Durham*, Kevin Costner

9. Rick's Café Américain, *Casablanca*, "As Time Goes By,"
    Humphrey Bogart, Lauren Bacall, Ingrid Bergman, Roberto
    Rossellini, Isabella Rossellini

10. Jennifer Lopez (J. Lo), Marc Anthony, Ben Affleck, Matt
    Damon, Jennifer Garner, *Juno*

11. Seersucker, Robert Preston, *The Music Man*, "76 Trombones,"
    Ron Howard, *Cocoon*, *Splash*, *The Little Mermaid*

12. Giselle Bundchen, Tom Brady, Leonardo DiCaprio, Munchkins,
    The Wizard of Oz, Toto, Kansas

13. Kevin Spacey, *American Beauty*, Warren Beatty, Annette Bening,
    Bugsy

14. *Eternal Sunshine of the Spotless Mind*, Kate Winslet, Jim Carrey

15. *Don't Mess with the Zohan*, Lindsay Lohan, Adam Sandler,
    "Hanukkah Song"

16. Bruce Willis, *The Sixth Sense*, *Night of the Living Dead*, Barbra
    Streisand

17. Daisy, Rose, Gertrude Stein, "Rose is a rose," Rosebud, *Citizen
    Kane*, Orson Welles, Chicken Little, "The sky is falling"

Score: _____

Take 10: Movies You've Probably Seen 1

1. *Taxi Driver*
2. *Jerry Maguire*
3. *Star Wars*
4. *The Silence of the Lambs*
5. *Dr. Strangelove*
6. *The Graduate*
7. *Five Easy Pieces*
8. *Apocalypse Now*
9. *Field of Dreams*
10. *Titanic*

Score: _____

Take 10: Movies You've Probably Seen II

1. *Ratatouille*
2. *10*
3. *There's Something About Mary*
4. *Fatal Attraction*
5. *Shrek*
6. *On the Waterfront*
7. *Invasion of the Body Snatchers*
8. *Forrest Gump*
9. *Easy Rider*
10. *Lawrence of Arabia*

Score: _____

Tongue Tipper: Wide World of Sports

1. Lou Gehrig
2. Muhammad Ali, Thrilla in Manila, Rumble in the Jungle, George Foreman
3. Luge, Curling, Shuffleboard, Carnival
4. A-Rod (Alex Rodriguez), Kabbalah, Madonna
5. Canoe, Kayak, Salma Hayek
6. Pilates, Spinning, Tour de France, Steroids
7. Sumo Wrestling, Summa cum Laude
8. Fly-fishing, *A River Runs Through It*, *On Golden Pond*, Henry Fonda, Katharine Hepburn
9. Michael Vick, Vick's, Pit Bulls, PETA
10. Jesse Ventura, Arnold Schwarzenegger, Hulk Hogan, *The Incredible Hulk*
11. Lacrosse, Lacoste, Polo
12. Beagle, Charles Darwin, Westminster Kennel Club, NASCAR
13. "Billie Jean," Billie Jean King, Chris Evert, Martina Navratilova
14. MSG, Madison Square Garden, New York Knicks, Spike Lee

Score: _____

SOUND ALIKES I

1. Pencil, Stencil, Stossel, Fossil
2. Piñata, Posada, Sonata, Sinatra
3. Muumuu, Choo-choo, Cashew, Achoo
4. Beanie, Bunny, Bonnie, Bony
5. Bib, Bob, Boob, Butt
6. Asia, Anastasia, Anesthesia, Amnesia
7. Wicca, Wikipedia, Wisteria, Hysteria
8. Planetarium, Sanitarium, Vegetarian, Samaritan
9. Pizza, Pisa, Pistachio, DiMaggio

Score: _____

Tongue Tipper: Superstars More or Less

1. Bruce Willis, *Die Hard*, Demi Moore, Ashton Kutcher
2. Ellen Barkin, *Sea of Love*, Ron Perelman
3. Tatum O'Neal, *Paper Moon*, Ryan O'Neal, Farrah Fawcett, John McEnroe
4. Ted Turner, Jane Fonda, CNN, Atlanta, *Gone With the Wind*, Rhett Butler, Scarlett O'Hara, "Frankly, my dear, I don't give a damn."
5. Alec Baldwin, Kim Basinger, *L.A. Confidential*, Ireland, *30 Rock*, Tina Fey, Sarah Palin, *Mean Girls*
6. Lance Bass, 'N Sync, Lance Armstrong, Sheryl Crow
7. Siegfried and Roy, Roy
8. Ivana Trump, Ivanka, Donald Trump, Melania Knauss, Barron
9. Nicole Kidman, Sunday
10. Angelina Jolie, Jennifer Aniston, Brad Pitt, Shiloh
11. Gwyneth Paltrow, Shakespeare, *Shakespeare in Love*, Apple
12. Michael Jackson, Prince Michael, Prince
13. Demi Moore, *Vanity Fair*, Rumer
14. Frank Zappa, Moon Unit Zappa

15. Katie Holmes, Tom Cruise, Suri, *Oklahoma!*, Corn, Elephant
16. Marilyn Monroe, Joe DiMaggio, "Mrs. Robinson", Simon & Garfunkel, Arthur Miller, *Death of a Salesman*, John Kennedy, Robert Kennedy
17. Heidi Klum, *Project Runway*, Seal, Heather Mills, Paul McCartney
18. Goldie Hawn; Kate Hudson; Owen Wilson; *You, Me, and Dupree*
19. Renée Zellweger, Kenny Chesney, *Bridget Jones's Diary*, Hugh Grant
20. Kirk Douglas, Michael Douglas, Catherine Zeta-Jones, *Chicago*
21. Lionel Richie, Nicole Richie, *The Simple Life*, Paris Hilton
22. The Dalai Lama, Tibet, Richard Gere
23. Sacha Baron Cohen, *Borat*, Sasha Cohen

Score: _____

Take 10: Flaming Redheads

1. The Weasley Family
2. Woody Allen
3. Marcia Cross
4. David Caruso
5. Debra Messing
6. Raggedy Ann
7. Lucy, or Lucille Ball
8. Carol Burnett
9. Ronald McDonald
10. Wendy

Score: _____

Take 10: Guys in White Suits

1. Colonel Sanders
2. Ricardo Montalban
3. Hervé Villechaize
4. Tom Wolfe
5. The Lone Ranger
6. John Travolta
7. Steve Martin
8. The Good Humor Man
9. Mark Twain
10. Osama bin Laden

Score: _____

Take 10: Guys with Mustaches

1. Teddy Roosevelt
2. Salvador Dalí
3. Groucho Marx
4. Albert Einstein
5. Ned Flanders
6. Juan Valdez
7. Adolf Hitler
8. Saddam Hussein
9. Fidel Castro
10. Charlie Chaplin

Score: _____

Tongue Tipper: Can't Stop the Beat

1. Mariah Carey, Tommy Mottola, Motorola, *Glitter*, Elvis
2. Mariachis, Sombreros, Margaritas

3. ABBA, *Mamma Mia!*, Meryl Streep, Pierce Brosnan, "S.O.S."

4. Boy George, George Michael, Larry Craig, Idaho

5. Christie Brinkley, Billy Joel, "Uptown Girl," Peter Cook

6. Jessica and Ashlee Simpson, O. J. Simpson

7. Billy Rae Cyrus, "Achy Breaky Heart," *Dancing with the Stars*, Miley Cyrus, *Hannah Montana*, Annie Leibovitz

8. Bob Marley, Jamaica, Reggae, Rastafarian, *Marley and Me*

9. *High School Musical*, *Romeo and Juliet*, *West Side Story*, Disney

10. Isadora Duncan, Dunkin' Donuts, Martha Graham, Graham Cracker

11. Jimmy Buffet, Warren Buffet, Omaha, *The New Yorker*

12. *Evita*, "Don't Cry for Me, Argentina," Madonna, Antonio Banderas

13. *Nashville*, *Grand Ole Opry*, Carrie Underwood, Dolly Parton, Dollywood, Robert Altman

14. "Reveille," Bugle, Bugles, Cheetos

15. Christina Aguiliera, MTV Awards, Madonna and Britney Spears

16. Accordion, Lawrence Welk

Score: _____

SOUND ALIKES II

1. Crack, Crick, Crock, Croak

2. Hockey, Hooky, Holy, Mole-y

3. Peyton, Putin, Puttin,' Putty

4. Knock-knock, Knick-knack, Kit Kat, Tic Tac

5. Eloise, Heloise, Christmas Trees, Lyme Disease

6. Torpedo, Toledo, Mosquito, Dorito

7. Ms., *Les Mis*, Lamaze, Llamas

8. Ruffles, Rifles, Truffles, Trifles

9. Academia, Macadamia, Macaroni, Macaroon

Score: _____

Tongue Tipper: History the Way We Remember It

1. Ben Franklin, Philadelphia, Liberty Bell, Boston, Paul Revere, The British

2. FDR, Eleanor Roosevelt, WWII, Pearl Harbor, Hawaii, Japanese

3. Deep Throat, Woodward and Bernstein, Watergate, Robert Redford, Dustin Hoffman

4. General Custer, Colonel Sanders, Sitting Bull, Little Big Horn, Wounded Knee

5. Charleston, Speakeasies, Prohibition, Depression, Hobos

6. John Adams, John Quincy Adams, George H.W. Bush and George W. Bush

7. Rosa Parks, Civil Rights, "I have a dream," Lincoln Memorial, Penny

8. Charles Lindbergh, Amelia Earhart, Bermuda Triangle, Hawaiian

9. Geronimo; *Fort Apache*, *The Bronx*; Paul Newman

10. John Hancock, Declaration of Independence, Fourth of July

11. Fifth Amendment, Chanel No. 5, Bill of Rights

12. Ticonderoga, Benedict Arnold, Ethan Allen

13. Flamingo, Florida, Al Gore, *An Inconvenient Truth*, Nobel Prize

14. Ronald Reagan, Mikhail Gorbachev, "Tear down this wall," George H. W. Bush, "Read my lips"

15. Harriet Beecher Stowe, *Uncle Tom's Cabin*, Harriet Tubman, Underground Railroad, Abraham Lincoln, Emancipation Proclamation

16. Vikings, Minnesota, Al Franken

17. Christopher Columbus; *Nina*, *Pinta*, and *Santa Maria*; Pilgrims; *Mayflower*; Plymouth

18. Socrates, Hemlock, Heimlich

19. Arthur, Round Table, *Camelot*, Robert Goulet, Sir Lancelot

20. Siberia, Solzenitzyn, Lenin, John Lennon

21. "Guantanamera," Guantánamo, Abu Ghraib, Water-boarding

22. Napoleon, Tiramisu, Mascarpone, Al Capone

23. Encyclopedia Britannica, Britain, Prince Charles, Princess Diana, Elton John, "Candle in the Wind"

24. Morse, Pigeons, *The Birdman of Alcatraz*

25. Julius Caesar, Cleopatra, Brutus, Anchovy

Score: _____

Take 10: Famous Generals

1. General Patton
2. General Mills
3. General Electric
4. General MacArthur
5. General Motors
6. General Eisenhower
7. *General Hospital*
8. General Store
9. General Admission
10. Surgeon General

Score: _____

Take 10: Presidential Losers

1. John Kerry, Teresa Heinz Kerry
2. John Edwards
3. Thomas E. Dewey
4. Hillary Clinton
5. Al Gore
6. Bob Dole
7. Michael Dukakis, Olympia Dukakis
8. Ross Perot
9. Howard Dean
10. Rudy Giuliani

Score: _____

Tongue Tipper: Animal Planet

1. Komodo; Kimono; Puff; Peter, Paul, and Mary; "If I Had a Hammer"; "Michael, Row the Boat Ashore"
2. Charlotte, Black Widow, Wilbur, *Charlotte's Web*, E. B. White, *Babe*
3. The Caterpillar Company, *The Very Hungry Caterpillar*, John Deere, Deer
4. Jane Goodall, Jane, Chimpanzees, *Bedtime for Bonzo*, Ronald Reagan
5. Koala, Eucalyptus, Menthol, Salem
6. Mustang, Pinto, Ralph Nader
7. Persian, Pekingese, Peking
8. Hippopotamus, Rhinoceros, Rhinoplasty
9. Loch Ness Monster, Bigfoot, Sasquatch, Satchmo, Louis Armstrong
10. Kobe, Kobe Bryant, Los Angeles Lakers, Kareem Abdul-Jabbar, Magic Johnson
11. Betas (Siamese Fighting Fish), Milk Bones, Alpo, Publishers Clearinghouse

Score: _____

SOUND ALIKES III

1. Pied Piper, Peter Piper, Peter Parker, Peter Peter
2. Scooby, Scrabble, Scribble, Squanto
3. Hooker, Hacker, Hiker, Heckler
4. Rubies, Rabies, Rabbis, Rib Eyes
5. Mormon, Merman, Mermaid, Meter Maid
6. Crater, Critter, Crichton, Crouton
7. Duck, Puck, Puke, Duke
8. Dolly, Polly, Molly, Holly
9. Blogger, Jogger, Juggler, Smuggler

Score: _____

Tongue Tipper: Page-Turners

1. *On Walden Pond*, Henry David Thoreau, Ralph Waldo Emerson, *Where's Waldo?*

2. *The Worst-Case Scenario Survival Handbook*, Steve Irwin, Paul Hogan, *The Crocodile Hunter*

3. Tennessee Williams, *A Streetcar Named Desire*, New Orleans, Katrina, FEMA, Mardi Gras, Rio de Janeiro

4. Harpoon, *Moby Dick*, *Jaws*, Manatees, Dolphins

5. Huckleberry Finn, Mississippi, Jim, Tom Sawyer, Mark Twain, Shania Twain

6. Raven, Edgar Allen Poe, Baltimore, Orioles

7. *A Million Little Pieces*, James Frey, Oprah Winfrey, *Larry King Live*, Pontiacs

8. Agatha Christie, *Murder on the Orient Express*, Hercule Poirot, Clue, Mustard

9. *The Far Side*, Gary Larson, Scott Adams, *Dilbert*, Garry Trudeau, *Doonesbury*

10. Albatross, Ancient Mariner, Hester Prynne, *The Scarlet Letter*, A

11. Robert Frost, "The Road Not Taken," *The Road Less Traveled*, Deepak Chopra, Okra

12. Tom Clancy, *The Hunt for Red October*, Sean Connery, Harrison Ford

13. *Little House on the Prairie*, *A Prairie Home Companion*, Garrison Keillor, Lake Wobegon

Score: _____

Take 10: Poets from A to Z

1. Sylvia Plath
2. Geoffrey Chaucer
3. Emily Dickenson
4. T. S. Eliot

5. e e cummings
6. Maya Angelou
7. Charles Osgood
8. Walt Whitman
9. Allen Ginsberg
10. Dorothy Parker

Score: _____

Take 10: Magazines, Etc.

1. *Sports Illustrated*
2. *Martha Stewart Living*
3. *People*
4. *Us*
5. *InStyle*
6. *Forbes*
7. *Seventeen*
8. *TV Guide*
9. *Readers Digest*
10. *National Geographic*

Score: _____

Tongue Tipper: What's in Store

1. Victoria's Secret, Brazil, Planters, Mr. Peanut
2. 7-Eleven, Big Gulps, Slurpees
3. William H. Macy, *Macy's*, *Miracle on 34th Street*, *It's a Wonderful Life*, James Stewart
4. Target, Kmart, Sears, Craftsman
5. Cadillac, Escalade, Hybrids, Prius, Whole Foods
6. LL Bean, LL Cool J, Lands' End

7. Home Depot, Costco, Wal-Mart, Sam Walton, the Waltons

8. Hammock, Hammacher-Schlemmer, Neiman Marcus

9. Amazon, Piranha, Leeches

10. A&P, AP (Advanced Placement), Brown, Wellesley, Wesley

11. Woolworth's, Woolite

12. Tiffany's, *Breakfast at Tiffany's*, "Moon River," Audrey Hepburn, Truman Capote, *In Cold Blood*

Score: _____

SOUND ALIKES IV

1. Pitter-patter, Mad Hatter, Switch Hitter, Babysitter

2. Timber, Timberlake, Timbaland, Switzerland

3. Stiletto, Staccato, Tomato, Tomahto

4. Puma, Uma, Rumor, Boomer

5. Makeup, Checkup, Tune-up, Pre-nup

6. Humpty-Dumpty, Hara-kiri, Halle Berry, Hail Mary

7. Basinette, Raisinette, Kitchenette, Cate Blanchett

8. Crooner, Crocker, Cracker, Quacker

9. TMZ, TMJ, DMZ, DNA

Score: _____

Tongue Tipper: On the Air

1. Elizabeth Hasselbeck, Tim Hasselbeck, *Survivor*, *The View*, Barbara Walters, Starr Jones

2. CPR, NPR, *Car Talk*

3. Mary Tyler Moore, *The Dick Van Dyke Show*, *Mary Poppins*, "Supercalifragilisticexpialidocious"

4. Dr. Laura Schlessinger, Rush Limbaugh, Don Imus, Rutgers, New Jersey, James McGreevey

5. *Two and a Half Men*, Charlie Sheen, Denise Richards, Richie Sambora, Heather Locklear

6. Anne Heche, Ellen DeGeneres, Portia de Rossi, *Ally McBeal*, Calista Flockhart

7. HBO, *Entourage*, *Big Love*, *The Wire*, *The Sopranos*, James Gandolfini, Edie Falco, Lorraine Bracco

8. Katie Couric, *The Today Show*, Bryant Gumbel, Greg Gumbel, Matt Lauer, Walter Cronkite, *CBS Evening News*

9. Jerry Springer, Maury Povich, *Tuesdays with Morrie*, Mitch Albom

10. Roulette, *Wheel of Fortune*, Vanna White, Pat Sajak, Bob Barker, *The Price Is Right*

11. Ryan Seacrest, Simon Cowell

12. Danny Bonaduce, *The Partridge Family*, *The Brady Bunch*

13. Steve Jobs, Steve Wozniak, Kathy Griffin, Sarah Silverman, Jimmy Kimmel

14. Anderson Cooper, Gloria Vanderbilt

15. Manolo Blahniks, Sarah Jessica Parker, *Sex and the City*, Cosmopolitan, *Ladies' Home Journal*, *Good Housekeeping*

Score: _____

Take 10: Cable News Guys

1. Lou Dobbs
2. Bill O'Reilly
3. Keith Olbermann
4. Wolf Blitzer
5. Maria Bartiromo
6. Chris Matthews, *Hardball*
7. Jim Cramer
8. Donny Deutsch
9. Paula Zahn
10. Mike and Mike

Score: _____

Take 10: Celebrity Chefs

1. Julia Child
2. Fannie Farmer
3. Rachael Ray
4. Paula Deen
5. Jamie Oliver
6. Emeril Lagasse
7. Giada de Laurentiis, Dino de Laurentiis
8. Padma Lakshmi, Salman Rushdie
9. Rocky Aoki, Benihana
10. Chef Boyardee

Score: _____

Tongue Tipper: Art History 101

1. Leroy Neiman, Leonard Nimoy
2. Jackson Pollock; Jackson Hole, Wyoming; Yellowstone National Park; Old Faithful
3. Hallmark, La-Z-Boy Recliner, Pipe, Norman Rockwell
4. Vincent van Gogh, "Vincent (Starry, Starry Night)," Don McLean, "American Pie," Tara Reid
5. Marc Chagall, Cirque du Soleil, Celine Dion
6. Stalactite, Stalagmite, Carlsbad Caverns, New Mexico, Georgia O'Keeffe, Frida Kahlo, Mexico
7. Michelangelo, *David*, Goliath
8. Reuben, Rubens
9. Roy Lichtenstein, Liechtenstein, Luxembourg, Lux
10. Andy Warhol, Studio 54, Hospital

Score: _____

SOUND ALIKES V

1. Diesel, Dazzle, Damsel, Denzel
2. Twister, Sister, Spritzer, Spitzer
3. Spanish, Spinach, Gingrich, Guinness
4. Valium, Vatican, Vitamin, Vietnam
5. Rigby, Rugby, Ripley, Wrigley
6. Croquet, Croquette, Crew Cut, Cold Cut
7. Rickets, Racquets, Rockettes, Rockets
8. Balloons, Baboons, Bassoons, Bazooms
9. Manga, Mangia, Mango, Tango

Score: _____

Tongue Tipper: All Over the Map

1. South Dakota, Mt. Rushmore
2. San Francisco, Tony Bennett, Rice-A-Roni
3. Pamplona, Ernest Hemingway, Kilimanjaro, Marlin, Marlon Brando
4. Lake Erie
5. Dover, Sole, English Channel, Stonehenge, The Rolling Stones, Mick Jagger
6. Niagara Falls, Viagra
7. Houston, Astrodome, Enron, Ken Lay
8. Holland, Belgium, Brussels, Brussels Sprouts, Flemish, Phlegm
9. Jim Morrison, Paris, Édith Piaf, Jerry Garcia, Cherry Garcia, Ben & Jerry
10. Myanmar, Mylar
11. Maple, Canada, Maple Syrup, Waffles
12. Amish, Quakers, Hasids, Buggies
13. Rome, Italy, Venice, Gondolas, Venison
14. Manila, Philippines, Imelda Marcos
15. Chile, Chili, Lima, Peru

16. Vienna, Austria, Switzerland, Swiss Army, Swiss, Heidi, Yodel
17. Calcutta, Mother Teresa, Leprosy, Leprechauns

Score: _____

Take 10: Greats

1. Alexander the Great
2. The Great Wall
3. Great Adventure, or Great America
4. *The Great Escape*
5. Great Dane
6. The Great Depression
7. "Great Balls of Fire"
8. The Greatest Show on Earth
9. The Greatest
10. The Great Houdini

Score: _____

Take 10: Magnificent Sevens

1. The Seven Dwarves
2. The Seven Deadly Sins
3. *Seven Brides for Seven Brothers*
4. *Seventh Heaven*
5. Seven-Year Itch
6. Seventh-Day Adventists
7. *The Seven Samurai*
8. *The Seven Habits of Highly Effective People*
9. George Carlin's "Seven Words You Can't Say on TV"
10. Seventh Inning Stretch

Score: _____

Tongue Tipper: Kids' Stuff

1. Mercury, Pluto, Goofy, Mickey, Donald
2. Cymbals; Triangle; "Twinkle, Twinkle Little Star"; "Bah, Bah Black Sheep"
3. Jack Sprat, Mother Goose, The Brothers Grimm, *Little Red Riding Hood, Hansel and Gretel*
4. Barney, Bert and Ernie, PBS, Tinky Winky the Teletubby
5. Jimmy Olsen, *The Daily Planet*, Jiminy Cricket, *Pinocchio*
6. Bratwurst, Bratz, American Girl, Kit Kittredge, Abigail Breslin
7. Brontosaurus, Fred, *The Flintstones*, Pebbles
8. Mr. Potato Head, *Toy Story*, Buzz Lightyear, Tim Allen
9. Robin Hood, Peter Pan, Tinkerbell, Paris Hilton
10. Rubber Cement, Compass, Protractor, Geometry
11. *Highlights*, *Mad Magazine*, Alfred E. Newman, Dave Letterman, Conan O'Brien, Jay Leno

Score: _____

SOUND ALIKES VI

1. Yahoo!, Yoo-Hoo, Voodoo, Boo-Boo
2. Alamo, Alimony, Palimony, Palomino
3. Ellis, Alice, Atlas, Hatless
4. Ding-Dong, Ping Pong, Singsong, *King Kong*
5. Jones, Joan, Jonas, Jonah
6. Greece, Geese, Geezer, Geyser
7. Ritz, Rats, Brits, Brats
8. Roth, Ruth, Wreath, Wrath
9. Bingo, Bongo, Bimbo, Limbo

Score: _____

Tongue Tipper: Science Fair

1. Anthrax, Amtrak

2. Sir Isaac Newton, Apple, Fig Newton

3. *Sybil*, *A Beautiful Mind*, Russell Crowe, Bipolar, Polar Bears

4. *Apollo 11*, Neil Armstrong, "One small step for (a) man, one giant leap for mankind," *Apollo 13*, Tom Hanks, Kevin Bacon

5. Tarot, Crystal Ball, Aquarius, Saturn, Pisces

6. Linus, Linus Pauling, Echinacea, Euthanasia

7. Four-Leaf Clover, Poison Ivy, Calamine Lotion, Columbine

8. Beriberi, Tsetse

9. Metamorphic, *The Metamorphosis*, Franz Kafka, *Catcher in the Rye*, J. D. Salinger

10. Centipede, Centimeter, Metric

11. Hypochondriacs, Placebo, Placido Domingo

Score: _____

Take 10: Is There a Doctor in the House?

1. Dr. Seuss

2. Dr. Scholl's

3. Dr. Spock

4. Dr. Jekyll

5. Dr. No

6. Dr. Doolittle

7. Dr. Phil

8. Dr. Dre

9. Dr. Watson

10. Dr Pepper

Score: _____

Take 10: Greek Myths and Legends

1. Cupid
2. Zeus
3. Hercules
4. Atlas
5. Pandora
6. Achilles
7. Apollo
8. Hermes
9. Poseidon
10. Cyclops

Score: _____

Tongue Tipper: Good Eats

1. Milky Way, Three Musketeers, Mouseketeers
2. Baguette, Croissant, Berets, Marcel Marceau
3. Jenny Craig, Kirstie Alley, *Cheers*, Valerie Bertinelli, Bertoli, Eddie van Halen, Queen Latifah
4. Grape-Nuts, Granola, Shredded Wheat
5. Turkey, Ottoman, Greece
6. Eskimo Pie, Eskimos, Igloos, Blubber, Balto
7. Mrs. Fields, Auntie Anne's, Sara Lee
8. Perrier, Pellegrino, Poland Spring, Fiji
9. Pomegranate, Methuselah, Abel, Cain
10. Engelbert Humperdinck, Pumpernickel
11. Fondue Kit, Sterno, Howard Stern
12. Fettuccine, Alfredo, Alfa Romeo
13. Triscuit

Score: _____

Sound Alikes VII

1. Neon, Freon, Peon, Leon
2. Lindbergh, *Hindenburg*, Limburger, Hamburger
3. Yoda, Yoga, Yogi, Hoagie
4. Teepee, Toupee, Tupac, Toothpick
5. Volvo, Frodo, Dodo, Pogo
6. Kryptonite, Samsonite, Dynamite, Vegemite
7. Aspirin, Aspen, Baskin, Bacon
8. Rodeo, Radio, Oreo, Oregano
9. Capote, Coyote, Peyote, *Jean Brodie*

Score: _____

Tongue Tipper: Gifts, Games, Gadgets, and Stuff

1. Timex, Rolex, Rolaids
2. Axe, Old Spice
3. Pinball, Jukebox, Willie Nelson, Bruce Springsteen, E Street Band
4. Sprinkler, Harp, Elizabeth Smart
5. Sudoku, Crossword Puzzle
6. Typewriter, Carbon Paper, Wite-Out
7. Monopoly, Boardwalk and Park Place, B&O
8. Cat's Cradle, Kurt Vonnegut, Joseph Heller, *Catch-22*
9. *Grand Theft Auto*, *The Simpsons*, Homer, *The Iliad*, *The Odyssey*
10. Mahjong, Jell-O

Score: _____

Take 10: Name That Game Show

1. *Jeopardy!*
2. *Family Feud*
3. *Are You Smarter Than a Fifth Grader?*

4. *The Moment of Truth*
5. *Who Wants to Be a Millionaire?*
6. *Deal or No Deal*
7. *The $64,000 Question*
8. *The Dating Game*
9. *The Newlywed Game*
10. *Hollywood Squares*

Score: _____

Take 10: Games People Play

1. Tetherball
2. Volleyball
3. Frisbee
4. Hopscotch
5. Monkey in the Middle
6. Hide and Go Seek
7. Pin the Tail on the Donkey
8. Dodgeball
9. Football
10. Marco Polo

Score: _____

Lightning Round: The One That's Not

Round I

1. Anorexia
2. Guinea Pig
3. Stephen Colbert
4. Date
5. Clam

6. CNN

7. Hare Krishnas

8. Yu-Gi-Oh

9. Robert Redford

10. Venus

11. Granite

12. Murder

13. Astrology

14. Debit

15. Mumps

16. Johnson

17. Louise

18. Digital

19. Bologna

20. Jerry Lewis

Score: _____

Round II

1. Samson

2. Anchovies

3. Da Vinci

4. Iceland

5. Stanley

6. Harvard

7. Chess

8. Trumpet

9. Greek

10. Alaska

11. The History Channel

12. Fore

13. Sickle

14. Homogeneous

15. Odometer

16. Yin
17. Ibuprofen
18. Newton
19. Hershey's
20. Antarctica

Score: _____

Round III

1. Davy Crockett
2. Bay of Pigs
3. Dubai
4. UPS
5. *Time*
6. Viola
7. Sasha
8. *Bewitched*
9. Cake
10. The Mississippi River
11. Pancakes
12. FBI
13. Machu Picchu
14. Comet
15. Czechoslovakia
16. Strom Thurmond
17. Gonorrhea
18. Portland
19. Monet
20. Rita Moreno

Score: _____

Round IV

1. *Penthouse*
2. Centigrade (Celsius)
3. Macarena
4. Skippy
5. Cantaloupe
6. Wine
7. Alligator
8. Vampire
9. Lassie
10. Aunt Jemima
11. Viral
12. Slate.com
13. Fauna
14. Sashimi
15. Beaver
16. Tolstoy
17. Dracula
18. The Tropic of Capricorn
19. Fannie Mae
20. Ricardo Montalban

Score: _____

Ready to write your own great
TONGUE TIPPERS, SOUND ALIKES,
TAKE 10s, and **THE ONE THAT'S NOTs?**
Jot them down here and try them out on
your friends! Then, if you'd like, send them
to us at www.whostheblondebook.com,
and we'll try to use them
in our next round!

★ Tongue Tipper ★

1. Who's the _____
_____
_____
_____
_____
_____

2. Who's the _____
_____
_____
_____
_____
_____

3. Who's the _____
_____
_____
_____
_____
_____

★ SOUND ALIKES ★

Fill in the blanks with words that sound alike, more or less. Sometimes less. Don't forget to include the answers!

1. _____
   _____
   _____
   _____
   _____
   _____
   _____
   _____

2. _____
   _____
   _____
   _____
   _____
   _____
   _____
   _____

3. _____
   _____
   _____
   _____
   _____
   _____
   _____

★ **Take 10** ★

What's—

1. The _____?

2. The _____?

3. The _____?

4. The _____?

5. The _____?

6. The _____?

7. The _____?

8. The _____?

9. The _____?

10. The _____?

⋆ The One That's Not ⋆

What's—

1. The _____?
   ONE THAT'S NOT . . .

2. The _____?
   ONE THAT'S NOT . . .

3. The _____?
   ONE THAT'S NOT . . .

4. The _____?
   ONE THAT'S NOT . . .

5. The _____?
   ONE THAT'S NOT . . .

6. The _____?
   ONE THAT'S NOT . . .

7. The _____?
   ONE THAT'S NOT . . .

8. The _____?
   ONE THAT'S NOT . . .

9. The _____?
   ONE THAT'S NOT . . .

10. The _____?
    ONE THAT'S NOT . . .